**W9-CUA-356**

1/88

# NEW POEMS

*By American Poets*

# By Rolfe Humphries

THE LOW PRICE OF THIS NEW COLLECTION IS MADE POS-
SIBLE BY LARGE PRINTINGS OF COMBINED EDITIONS.

# NEW
# POEMS
## By American Poets

---

Edited by ROLFE HUMPHRIES

BALLANTINE BOOKS · NEW YORK · 1953

"The Ash and the Oak," and "The True Weather for Women," by Louis Simpson, appeared in *American Scholar*, Copyright 1951 by The United Chapters of Phi Beta Kappa. "Vacation Trip," by Donald C. Babcock, appeared in *American Weave*, Copyright 1952 by American Weave Press. "The Dance," by Theodore Roethke, appeared in *The Atlantic Monthly*, Copyright 1952 by Theodore Roethke. "Dream of a Decent Death," by G. A. Borgese, and "Apology," by Richard Wilbur, appeared in the *Beloit Poetry Journal*. "Olive Grove," by James Merrill, and "Leaves Before the Wind," by May Sarton, and "Beasts," by Richard Wilbur, appeared in *Botteghe Oscure*. "Degrees of Shade," by H. A. Pinkerton, appeared in the *Carmel Pine Cone*, Copyright 1950 by Wilma Cook and Clifford H. Cook. "The Library," by Mary Mills, appeared in the *Colorado Quarterly*, Copyright 1953 by the University of Colorado. "At Cambridge," by Audrey McGaffin, appeared in *Contact*. "The Human Being is a Lonely Creature," "Sainte Anne de Beaupre," and "Ur Burial" are printed here for the first time by permission of Richard Eberhart. "Ashokan," by Dachine Rainer, appeared in *Epoch*, Copyright 1952 by Epoch Associates. "The Sloth," by Theodore Roethke, appeared in *Flair*, Copyright 1950 by Theodore Roethke. "Billiards," by Walker Gibson, appeared in *Furioso*, Copyright 1948 by Reed Whittemore. "Processional," by William Jay Smith, appeared in *Harper's Bazaar*, Copyright 1950 by The Hearst Corporation. "Mrs. Severin," by Winfield Townley Scott, appeared in *The Hopkins Review*, Copyright 1951 by The Hopkins Review. "Song for the Squeeze-Box," by Theodore Roethke; and "Beasts," by Richard Wilbur, appeared in *The Hudson Review*, Vol. 5, No. 4, Winter 1953; and Vol. 6, No. 1, Spring, 1953, respectively, Copyright 1953 by The Hudson Review, Inc. "Song of Fixed Accord," "Two Illustrations That the World is What You Make of It," and "Prologues to What Is Possible," by Wallace Stevens, appeared in *The Hudson Review*, Vol. 5, No. 3, Autumn 1952, Copyright 1952 by Wallace Stevens. "Beaver Sign," by Kenneth Porter, appeared in *The Kansas Magazine*, Copyright 1953 by The Kansas Magazine Publishing Association. "First Song," by Galway Kinnell, Copyright 1953 by Galway Kinnell. "Woods," by W. H. Auden, appeared in *The Listener*. "The Final Green," by Leah Bodine Drake, appeared in *The Lyric*, Copyright 1951 by Virginia Kent Cummins.

The following poems appeared in *The Nation:* "Apparition of Splendor" (1952), by Marianne Moore; "This World" (1952), "Euroclydon" (1952), and "Return to Life" (1952), by Abbie Huston Evans; and "Prognostic" (1953) and "The Cloisters" (1953), by Samuel Yellen. The foregoing poems were copyrighted in the respective years shown by The Nation Associates, Inc.

"Thought for the Winter Season," by Mary Elizabeth Osborn, appeared in the *New Quarterly of Poetry*, Copyright 1948 by the New Quarterly of Poetry.

The following poems appeared in the *New York Herald Tribune:* "Ornamental Water" (1952), "Color Alone Can Speak" (1953), and

BALLANTINE BOOKS
404 FIFTH AVENUE, NEW YORK 18, N.Y.

# Contents

# *Introduction*

ALL OF THE POEMS in this collection were submitted
directly by the authors in response either to personal
invitations from the editor, a circular issued by the
publishers and mailed to as many authors as we could
reach, or a public notice which appeared in the Sunday
Book Review section of The New York Times. In
many cases, poets suggested to the editor the names of
other poets, or passed the word along to fellow writers,
so that the project, to a greater extent than is usual
with anthologies, became something of a co-operative
venture. What I am getting at is that this book is no
scissor-and-paste job, with the editor going through
current magazines, verse columns of newspapers, and,
above all, other anthologies.

The response, both in quantity and quality, sur-
passed all our expectations, and that is considerable f
an understatement. The amount of screwball material
was surprisingly low, and the number of persons who
failed to enclose return postage for the return of un-
acceptable manuscripts fell appreciably below actu-
arial estimates. It is true that reading, over a period of
several months an average of fifty manuscripts (some
of them book length) per week, the editor could, even
before opening the envelopes, anticipate certain pos-

sibilities, or trends; there were, in the main, two categories which proved repetitious and boring. These were: (A) the poem, usually rhymed, in which a lady had had the experience of seeing a star, followed, shortly, by having an ecstasy, rhyming, more often than not, with mem-o-ree or im-mor-tal-i-tee, in the last quatrain (this type of verse appears most often in little poetry magazines which do not pay); and (B) the poem, usually free verse, beginning with an arresting image in which, for example, "the fanged white cuspidors of the dawn spit at the neon morning," and along about the third or fourth line the author, usually a young man of forty, is contemplating himself in a mirror and having some very glum reflections indeed. (This type finds general acceptance in avant-garde periodicals of one kind or another and also in University Reviews, some of which do not pay either.) It is our belief that very few poems of Type A or Type B will be found in the following pages.

Our long and varied list of acknowledgments, however, is ample proof that American magazines, along with a certain amount of junk, manage, nevertheless, to print a substantial quality of viable poetry. Their task, day in, day out, is considerably more difficult than that of the anthologist, who takes on a job like this once in a blue moon, and the anthologist has, moreover, advantages on which it would not be decent to dwell. Poets, of course, are insatiable enough to wish that editors would do very much more for them than they do do; at the same time, they are not ungrateful for what is being done, and they are sometimes pleasantly surprised that it is as much as it is.

Still, it is not enough, in an anthology of this kind, to present a selection from the acceptable and printed verse of, say, the last five years. In our announcement to poets, we stated our feeling that the true state of American poetry today was by no means adequately reflected by the scope of the current market. This statement, obviously, committed us to finding poetry, good poetry, which had not seen print; our findings can be verified in this collection. Our book contains a great many poems, some by well known authors, which have not been previously published, and for several authors, half a dozen, more or less, this is a first appearance. In the editor's opinion, some of this work is as exciting and arresting as anything in the book; we are pleased and proud of the honor of presenting the poems of Ashton Greene, Annemarie Ewing, Richard Aldridge, Mary Mills, Richard Gillman, John Hay, and others, and we cheerfully admit that their presence is due as much to good luck as to good management. We really had no idea.

Statistics are not the most interesting matter for an introduction, and the reader who insists on them can compile his own data from the brief biographical notes which introduce each poet. Nevertheless, we might make one or two points. Geographically, this book is bounded on the northeast by New England, on the northwest by Washington and Oregon, on the southwest by California and Arizona, on the south by Louisiana and the Canal Zone. In time, there is a range of over five decades between the birth years of our oldest and youngest poet. We have tried to present no poet in smidgets, to give each time to be heard, never less than two pages, seldom more than five. We believe we have variety and interest; but that is really for the reader to judge.

Ours is—we know, we know—a Lost Generation, and this is An Age of Anxiety. Sheer swank, I sometimes think; we are giving ourselves airs. Or, at least, in the profession of anxiousness, there is an element of fashion, of chichi: how many, I wonder, who feel sure that the Atom Bomb is going to get us all tomorrow, ever dream about atom bombs, instead of their father chasing their mother with a knife, or vice versa? The world may be coming to an end any minute, but a good many of us, it seems, are going to have brand-new nylons, and if possible, an Overdrive Olds to go around in for a view of the ruins; anyhow, we all dash out to be vaccinated when a smallpox scare comes along. We really believe in life more than we say we do.

It would be false to say that there are no gloomy nor macabre poems in this collection, as it would have been false to see to it that all such were excluded. We have not, on the other hand, stacked the deck, but it has been reassuring to find so much evidence of health, high spirit, courage, humor, a preference for life as against its opposite number, and this includes a preference for living language as against senile cliches, moribund rhythms, and just plain dead words. "We believe," we said in our circular announcement to poets, "that there are new voices to be heard and that, in the face of an age of anxiety, many speak out still with vitality and affirmation; we reject the easy criticism that condemns all modern poetry as obscure, nervous, and morose verbalizing. We are confident that this anthology will amply demonstrate our belief and that every good poet in America will help us make good the demonstration." Well?

I must conclude with a grateful personal acknowledgment to Mrs. Marie Rodell, who was kind enough to put my name in nomination for this job. And I owe very much to the poets, rejected or accepted, who were my collaborators; they were generous in their offerings, patient with my delays and naggings, willing in their revisions, and most encouraging in their letters of warm-hearted appreciation. For their sake, I hope that we all have still to acknowledge one final debt of gratitude, to the reading public for the support which will make it possible to—shall we?—do this again some time.

ROLFE HUMPHRIES

# NEW POEMS

*By American Poets*

RICHARD ALDRIDGE, the youngest poet in this book, was born in New York City in 1930. He is a graduate of Amherst College, where he won the Colin Armstrong Poetry Prize, and now lives in Washington, where he is employed in government research. Except for appearances in *Context*, the Amherst College literary magazine, these poems are the first he has published.

>>>-->>>-->>>-->>>-->>>-->>>-->>>-->>>-->>>-->>>-->>>-<<<-<<<-<<<-<<<-<<<-<<<-<<<-<<<-<<<-<<<-<<<

## The Pine Bough

I saw a thing, and stopped to wonder—
For who had set the moment when
The pine bough should dip out from **under**
The white oppressor's arm of snow,
And upward fling itself, as though
Attracted to a blue May heaven?

## Spring Night

This mist has followed on an all-day rain.
It sustains the general wetness so, that
If it weren't for street-lamps stationed here
    and there,
Diffusing out their fuzz-edged clouds of light,
I'd think I'd come to take my nighttime **stroll**
Along the floor of some inhabitable sea.

As it is, forms so strangely cast invite
Marine imaginings. The high hedge down
    this lane
Is some outsized porifera. My hat
Is scraped by sunken spars, their mast a
    sodden tree.

1

In fact, I wish I had fins to control,
And through this gauze of haunted air
Go gliding, in staring fishlike stalking.
But I can't, you know; I have to keep on walking.

## A Matter of Life and Death

This watchful nurse and bundled boy at play
I designated to a Venice park
Decreeing the Quattrocento would do well.
Over there, a student on a cement bench
 Before the public library could tell
 (If asked) it was a toga that today
I clothed him in.  That soldier and his wench
Who lie embraced at dusk await the dark
Of an Egyptian night.

                                And so I turned around
The centuries, taunting down this twentieth.
To make such transfers without stir or sound
Of course meant open trafficking with Death.
But how could beings so wholly present-bound
Be made aware that I had stopped their breath?

## To Himself

Leave her now, go out and learn
To look ahead and see the years
That bring back sleep; no longer yearn
To grasp the riddle that beset
How many others in their turn,
The strange pandemic ill of love.

Agreeing, I cry I would, and yet
Around me sorrow's image clings:
I only see cold skies above
The promise that the crocus brings:
The rain, a blowing mist of tears;
The rose, that draws the touch, and stings.

KENNETH SLADE ALLING was born in Derby, Conn. He
has published one book of poems, *Core of Fire,* and his work
has also appeared in *Poetry,* and various other magazines. His
professional occupation is in the insurance field; his home in
Wilton, Conn.

## First World War

After the Armistice I was at Tours,
Where the girls grew on trees
And where the shaking of any bough would
    shower
You with dozens of these.

Were the gods good. In their ironic way.
Hyderabad's Nizam would,
Ancestrally schooled in the zenana, say
The gods were good.

Brought up by generations (as was I)
That came to a bleak coast,
And always under the surveillance of my
Grandfather's ghost,

I found the harem alien, troublesome,
And having it in haste,
Unmanageable. I was overcome
By the sudden East.

## Dead Wasp

The small wasp lies in state,
A formidable design in black and gold:
Tiered like a Chinese tower, his abdomen;
His wings as hyaline as heaven,
Windows the now elegiac light pours through.

3

## Onion Skin in Barn

It looks a piece of golden, broken glass,
This fragment here of what entire it was:
From a Venetian furnace long ago,
To set with strange light some king's room aglow.
But fallen on this drab and dusty floor
It has its palace as it had before.


## Monsoon

Walk in the half light of rain
Backwards
Into the rain
Of a rainy city.
It wasn't the destination, the terminal,
You fevered for then,
It was the ride in the *gharri,*
The smell of the bazaar
That stays with you;
It wasn't the girl,
It was the old horse
And the *gharri-wallah*
That your annas took.
Your annas bought more, it seems,
   than your rupees did
In lasting pleasure.
The rain came to the city in a *gharri* too,
That *gharri-wallah* kept his fare waiting.
You were the rain that wanted your city,
City in city,
The great city only the environs
Of your small intricate city,
And the *gharri* so slow in getting you there.

# On the Park Bench

On the park bench the man, alone,
Playing chess, "a game of pure skill."
He walks in a kingdom of diagonals
The moon's gravity orders his steps
The traffic is all of his own making, but
If he runs himself down
He won't die,
He'll only be deported.

# Dr. Donne

The grave came to him, at his wish, before
He could come to the grave and when he died
He did return the visit, nothing more;
The social debt to death was satisfied.

W. H. AUDEN was born in York, England, in 1907. He became an American citizen in 1939. He is the author of numerous books of poems, from *The Orators* to *The Age of Anxiety*, which won a Pulitzer Prize, and *Nones*. Most recently, in collaboration with Chester Kallman, he wrote the libretto for the Stravinsky opera, *The Rake's Progress*. Mr. Auden is a Fellow of the National Institute of Arts and Letters and at present lives in Northampton, Mass., where he holds a professorship at Smith College.

➤➤➤➤➤➤➤➤➤➤➤➤➤➤➤➤➤➤➤➤➤➤➤◄◄◄◄◄◄◄◄◄◄◄◄◄◄◄◄◄◄◄◄◄◄◄

## *Lakes*

A lake allows an average father, walking slowly,
    To circumvent it in an afternoon,
And any healthy mother to halloo the children
    Back to her bedtime from their games across:
(Anything bigger than that, like Michigan or Baikal,
    Though potable, is an 'estranging sea') .

Lake-folk require no fiend to keep them on their toes;
    They leave aggression to ill-bred romantics
Who duel with their shadows over blasted heaths:
    A month in a lacustrine atmosphere
Would find the fluvial rivals waltzing not exchanging
    The rhyming insults of their great-great-uncles.

No wonder Christendom did not get really started
    Till, scarred by torture, fresh from caves and jails,
Her pensive chiefs converged on the Ascanian Lake
    And by that stork-infested shore invented
The life of Godhead, making catholic the figure
    Of three small fishes in a triangle.

Sly Foreign Ministers should always meet beside one,
    For, whether they walk widdershins or deasil,
The path will yoke their shoulders to one liquid
    centre
    Like two old donkeys pumping as they plod;

6

Such physical compassion may not guarantee
        A marriage for their armies, but it helps.

Only a very wicked or conceited man,
        About to sink somewhere in mid-Atlantic,
Could think Poseidon's frown was meant for him in
                person,
        But it is only human to believe
The little lady of the glacier lake has fallen
        In love with the rare bather whom she drowns.

The drinking water of the city, where one panics
        At nothing noticing how real one is,
May come from reservoirs whose guards are all too
                conscious
        Of being followed: Webster's cardinal
Saw in a fish-pool something horrid with a hay-rake;
        I know a Sussex hammer-pond like that.

A haunted lake is sick, though; normally, they doctor
        Our tactile fevers with a visual world
Where beaks are dumb like boughs and faces safe
                like houses;
        The water-scorpion finds it quite unticklish,
And, if it shudder slightly when caressed by boats,
        It never asks for water or a loan.

Liking one's Nature, as lake-lovers do, benign
        Goes with a wish for savage dogs and man-traps:
One Fall, one dispossession, is enough I'm sorry;
        Why should I give Lake Eden to the Nation
Just because every mortal Jack and Jill has been
        The genius of some amniotic mere?

It is unlikely I shall ever keep a swan
        Or build a tower on any small tombolo,
But that's not going to stop me wondering which
                class
        Of lake I would decide on if I should.
Moraine, pot, oxbow, glint, sink, crater, piedmont,
        dimple. . . .
        Just reeling off the names is ever so comfy.

# Woods

Sylvan men at savage in those primal woods
Piero di Cosimo so loved to draw,
Where nudes, bears, lions, sows with women's heads
Mounted and murdered and ate each other raw,
Nor thought the lightning-kindled bush to tame
But, flabbergasted, fled the useful flame.

Reduced to patches owned by hunting squires
Of villages with ovens and a stocks,
They whispered still of most unsocial fires,
Though Crown and Mitre warned their silly flocks
The pasture's humdrum rhythms to approve
And to abhor the licence of the grove.

Guilty intention still looks for a hotel
That wants no details and surrenders none;
A wood is that, and throws in charm as well,
And many a semi-innocent, undone,
Has blamed its nightingales who round the deed
Sang with such sweetness of a happy greed.

Those birds, of course, did nothing of the sort,
And, as for sylvan nature, if you take
A snapshot at a picnic, O how short
And lower-ordersy the Gang will look
By those vast lives that never took another
And are not scared of gods, ghosts, or stepmother.

Among these coffins of its by-and-by
The Public can (it cannot on a coast)
Bridle its skirt-and-bargain-chasing eye,
And where should an austere philologist
Relax but in the very world of shade
From which the matter of his field was made.

Old sounds re-educate an ear grown coarse,
As Pan's green father suddenly raps out
A burst of undecipherable Morse,

And cuckoos mock in Welsh, and doves create
In rustic English over all they do
To rear their modern family of two.

Now here, now there, some loosened element,
A fruit in vigor or a dying leaf,
Utters its private idiom for descent,
And late man, listening through his latter grief,
Hears, close or far, the oldest of his joys,
Exactly as it was, the water noise.

A well-kempt forest begs Our Lady's grace;
Someone is not disgusted, or at least
Is laying bets upon the human race
Retaining enough decency to last;
The trees encountered on a country stroll
Reveal a lot about a country's soul.

A small grove massacred to the last ash,
An oak with heart-rot, give away the show:
This great society is going smash;
They cannot fool us with how fast they go,
How much they cost each other and the gods!
A culture is no better than its woods.

DONALD C. BABCOCK was born in Minneapolis, Minn., in 1885. He has published *Man and Social Achievement,* a study of social evolution, and won the Durham Poetry Award, given by the University of New Hampshire Writers' Conference for his brochure, *For Those I Taught. New England Harvest,* a volume of poems is scheduled for 1953 publication. Mr. Babcock is Professor of Philosophy at the University of New Hampshire, and lives in Durham, N. H.

## America

So, then, we were no new device at all,
We who were born the first-fruits of the West.
Or so we fancied. Oh, we stood so tall,
We looked abroad and smiled at all the rest:—
They dwelt in Europe's tombs, they dwelt in
    shadow;
Their forests fell in dust; mold and the blight
Lay on the vine; the moss crept on the meadow;
The doom had come on peasant, priest, and
    knight.
And over us, who would not stoop to glean
Among the echoes of their precious word,
Nor doubted that our liberty must mean
The advent of an ultimate accord,
Bides now an ignorance of all things old,
A famine of the heart, and bitter cold.

## The Anthill

The anthill lay unsheltered in the sun,
And all its populace ran out and in,
Looking for brave new projects to begin,
Though ignorant of those they had begun.

I moved my foot: they could not choose but run.
But when I heard the belfry making din
To call the hour across the wooded linn,
They nothing knew that half their day was done.
How strange if some dimension unconceived,
Indifferent to our space-bound sun and moon,
Held not a race who hardly sensed our laws—
Who for our fardels neither joyed nor grieved,
Yet took grave note, at some high, holy noon,
Of other bells than those that give us pause.


## Two Things

Two things were set
That I must learn
On earth, though tears be wet
And fire unstinting burn.
Seek through the flesh: you will not find
The living likeness of the mind;
Explore the mind: you will discern no trace
Of matter or its clinging shell of space.

This learned, pass on, and presently confess
That nerves lend action to your willfulness.
The boundaries of self evade
The searching of your careful blade.
Even to the very end,
And each by each refined,
The two will blend:
The flesh, the mind.


## Neoplatonic Soliloquy

The soul must have, for its great need,
An otherness on which to feed.
The soul must have, and this no less,
Surpassage of all otherness.

The soul within itself must see
Its ultimate identity,
And yet must find, as well, a friend
To be the meaning and the end,
So that the proof of self may be
 An infinite plurality.

Before the later shadows loom,
O Soul, within thine house make room.


# In A Garden

### (with the usual apologies)

I think that I shall never make
A poem sinuous as a snake:

A snake that can us mammals mock
Whenas he moves upon a rock;

Whose muscular and graceful strength
Dwells in the one dimension, length;

Who has no radiating limb
And yet on waves of land can swim;

Who can from raspberry vines and air
Devise himself a rocking-chair;

Who worships silent in the sun;
Who has no projects to be done;

Who thinks no thought, who makes no sound,
Preferring to remain profound;

Who, though from dust he scarce can rise,
Appropriates man's paradise.

I strive, like Adam, every spring,
To conjure that elusive thing,

An Eden, with my hoe and rake:
The Serpent only God could make.

# Vacation Trip

Some modest windfalls from the Tree
Of Paradise belong to me.
Now, parked in the September sun,
I watch the ticking meters run
With Time their swift deliberate race.
I stay here by a nickel's grace,
And watch the sidewalk's pageantry:
The windows of the A & P,
The sometime 'pothecary's shop
Where now the Boston buses stop,
The thoughtful child whose tongue has grown
Prehensile round the ice-cream cone,
The stop-sign tilted out of true
Where the great elm-roots shoulder through
To hint that wineglass elms may see
The day when motors cease to be,
And, free from apprehension, men
Can walk like villagers again,
Protected from too vast surmise
Under the Trees of Paradise.

# The Migrant

Close to the frontier of Eternity is my patrimony,
And I dwell there in a grandeur not wholly to my
    liking,
Since all children of the Eternal are strangely drawn
To play truant in the Temporal.

There is another demesne that lies next to this,
And I seem to have wandered witlessly into it,
Till I no longer know whether I am at home or
    abroad—
The tangled paths of Time.

13

Time's son lurks there, mischievous, mundane of
    spirit.
He is a fletcher by trade, and bowman betimes.
He sends unconsidered arrows slithering in the grass:
Now and again they mark me.

I feign not to notice him; I walk erect,
For I am man; the horizon is my destiny.
The plains of variance and vicissitude
Are foreground only.

Some day Time himself will string the bow
And aim a final shaft high at my heart.
It will not find me. I shall be even higher.
Past all chronometry.

CHARLES G. BELL was born in Greenville, Miss., in 1916. A graduate of the University of Virginia, he was also a Rhodes Scholar at Oxford. Mr. Bell has contributed essays on philosophical, literary, and political topics to *Common Cause, PMLA, The Journal of Comparative Literature,* and *Philosophy of Science;* his poetry has appeared in *Harper's Magazine, The Land, The Beloit Poetry Journal, The Nation,* and *New World Writing;* and a volume, *Songs for a New America,* will be published this fall by the University of Indiana Press. He is Assistant Professor of Humanities at the University of Chicago.

# Heraclitus in the West
*"The way up and the way down is the same"*

And the raying sun from behind breaks out east
Over the sea, opening a river of light
Into the dark of cloud and the wind-tossed gray;
Against that drop, the unguessed wheeling gulls
Burn silver sparks of search, volitional fire.

Once we looked west over sea to the golden
Oblate and beckoning sun dropping without cloud
Behind the fired earth's verge; and the call was
    sunward,
Burning rooks and gulls of the dark eastern land,
Stirred wings west up rivers of light from the gray.

Here the great sun drops at our backs behind us;
The call has been followed to the last verge of land,
The light struck and the wave rebounds; into dark
We burn down rivers of fire, re-entering cloud,
Gulls to the gray-walled close by the eastern sea.

Sunlight before or behind are tides of one motion;
The way up and down currents of the single sea;
Beyond east or west rounds the gulf of one darkness;
And every flight of spirit burns rivers of fire,
Gulls to the landless drop of the wind-gray cloud.

15

## This Little Vigil

Between the first pangs and the last of love
There is no difference, but that the first
Are bitter-sweet, the last are merely bitter.

Here in the waste of fore and after desert
The brief oasis of a trysting passage
Lures to the longed-for and regretted joys.


## Diretro al Sol

Over the gulf and soaring of the city
We came at dusk to the roof-garden rail.
Darkness flowed in the streets; the dream-world
   beauty
Of towered steel rose in the violet air—
Bands and heights of light under the sky's plumes;
Cars to the suburbs burn the long road lanes.

Here on the terrace, drinking wine and eating,
People of every nation, hearts unquelled
By the encroaching shadows, mingle, speaking
Tongues of kindred lands. Their voices tell
Of customs and of needs, of the fools who rule;
They are loose in talk and laughter, slurs and
   dreams.

And the clouds relinquish the sun's brown setting.
Twilight deepens as the city glows.
Out of the past of another world-evening
Spirit has suffered, a great voice looms;
It is Pericles—with Athens at the bourn
Of her adventurous sailing into ruin:

"We are the school of Hellas. Wonder unending
Of after ages will be ours. We have
Made sea and land the highway of our daring.

If now obedient to the general law
We invite decay, the greatness we have known
Will be some break of beauty in that gloom."

These words echo in the mind. From dark flashing
Along the gray shore and the wash of waves,
Towers, and cars streaming. Up vibrant air
   reaching
Cones of light catch at the destinate planes.
The roar west and east. Here in the hum
Of mingled voices careless freedom sings.

And we too have lived the dayspring and daring
That all time will remember; we have seen,
Over the earth-foreclosure of our wasting,
Still the incredible brightening of the dream . . .
Now promise is almost presence under the dome
Of night stirred with light and the rush of wings.

# *Woodbird*

Woodbird trilling softly from the autumn spray;
Red leaves above quiet waters
In the webs of sun.

This autumn is my spring: down the gold
   forest ways
Your frank eyes guide, the daughters
Of laughter run.

When I forget, my love, image of the light
   and spray,
Forget, eyes, earth and waters
And lose the sun.

# On a Baltimore Bus

Observing point by point mere instances
(As lice a courtesan) what can you see
Except this valueless: that what is, is,
And if flesh move, that's just its tendency?

A public carrier may be sold to some
Who fill a private purse; so placards press
From every surface—dentifrice and gum—;
Then radio's installed, public address,
And the hourly lechery of melodic sale.

Have all the annals of old tyrannies
Told such pervasion? No quiet intervale
Of private peace from prying enterprise?
Such usurpation?
                    These are the letters spread
That read the corporate virtue strumpeted.


# From Le Havre

The tug pulls, tightening the steel strand.
  This harbor
Water churns oil and chunks of bread. Slowly
Slowly the great ship moves. Strong is the land's
Hold. And the wharf is lined with waving hats
And hands. Strangers to me. And strangely sad
I wave—though the call of the west is calling
  me home.

Houseless home of our wandering—vacant fields
And tall inhuman cities. I would not turn.
But eyes go east and a face planned to be gay
Is quietly pensive, and the hand waves—as if
I were myself, waving myself good-bye,
The new waving to the old, and both alone.

Thought wins me back to a day closing a ride
Through German forests, wheat and vine, at
    cloistered
Maulbronn, where a crescent moon is the pearl
Of sunset, and the mingled glow, down pointed
Windows, lights from bowl to bowl its
    murmuring
Fountain, and the mystery of Gothic and
    water are one.

Birth and being define us home. But the harvest
Valleys and tender towns, the laughing virgins
In the carved stone—O they wrap round
    the heart;
(A few months only) and on this smooth-
    lipped land,
Like a remembered love we would long to
    hold,
Hold her forever and fasten the lips here.

Now the waving arms are gone, and the chapel
    under
The hill. A destiny of power takes
The hull. Wild whirls of water drive us on.
And the course is westward, where steel towers
    loom,
Larvae of the future, along the confluent
    streams,
On the leafwork of a continent axil and veins.

LOUISE BOGAN was born in 1897 in Livermore Falls, Maine. Author of four books of poetry, *Body of This Death, Dark Summer, The Sleeping Fury,* and *Poems and New Poems,* she has also published a prose study, *Achievement in American Poetry, 1900-1950.* Winner of numerous prizes, twice holder of a Guggenheim Fellowship, Miss Bogan has also served as Poetry Consultant to the Library of Congress, and is a member of the National Institute of Arts and Letters. She lives in New York City, and is Verse Critic on the staff of *The New Yorker.*

# After the Persian

## I

I do not wish to know
The depths of your terrible jungle:
From what nest your leopard leaps
Or what sterile lianas are at once your
    serpents' disguise and home.

I am the dweller on the temperate threshold,
The strip of corn and vine,
Where all is translucence (the light!),
Liquidity, and the sound of water.
Here the days pass under shade
And the nights have the waxing and the
    waning moon.
Here the moths take flight at evening;
Here at morning the dove whistles and
    the pigeons coo.
Here, as night comes on, the fireflies
    wink and snap
Close to the cool ground,
Shining in a profusion
Celestial or marine.

Here it is never wholly dark but always
    wholly green,
And the day stains with what seems to be
    more than the sun
What may be more than my flesh.

## II

I have wept with the spring storm;
Burned with the brutal summer.
Now, hearing the wind and the
    twanging bow-strings
I know what winter brings.

The hunt sweeps out upon the plain
And the garden darkens.
They will bring the trophies home
To bleed and perish
Beside the trellis and the lattices,
Beside the fountain, still flinging diamond
    water,
Beside the pool
(Which is eight-sided, like my heart).

## III

All has been translated into treasure:
Weightless as amber,
Translucent as the currant on the branch,
Dark as the rose's thorn.

Where is the shimmer of evil?
This is the shell's iridescence
And the wild bird's wing.

## IV

Ignorant, I took up my burden in the
    wilderness.
Wise with great wisdom, I shall lay it
    down upon flowers.

Goodbye, goodbye!
There was so much to love, I could not
    love it all;
I could not love it enough.

Some things I overlooked, and some I
    could not find.
Let the crystal clasp them
When you drink your wine, in autumn.


## Train Tune

Back through clouds
Back through clearing
Back through distance
Back through silence

Back through groves
Back through garlands
Back by rivers
Back below mountains

Back through lightning
Back through cities
Back through stars
Back through hours

Back through plains
Back through flowers
Back through birds
Back through rain

Back through smoke
Back through noon
Back along love
Back through midnight

# Song for the Last Act

Now that I have your face by heart, I look
Less at its features than its darkening frame
Where quince and melon, yellow as young flame,
Lie with quilled dahlias and the shepherd's
    crook.
Beyond, a garden. There, in insolent ease
The lead and marble figures watch the show
Of yet another summer loath to go
Although the scythes hang in the apple trees.

Now that I have your face by heart, I look.

Now that I have your voice by heart, I read
In the black chords upon a dulling page
Music that is not meant for music's cage,
Whose emblems mix with words that shake
    and bleed.
The staves are shuttled over with a stark
Unprinted silence. In a double dream
I must spell out the storm, the running stream.
The beat's too swift. The notes shift in the dark.

Now that I have your voice by heart, I read.

Now that I have your heart by heart, I see
The wharves with their great ships and archi-
    traves;
The rigging and the cargo and the slaves
On a strange beach under a broken sky.
O not departure, but a voyage done!
The bales stand on the stone; the anchor weeps
Its red rust downward, and the long vine creeps
Beside the salt herb, in the lengthening sun.

Now that I have your heart by heart, I see.

PHILIP BOOTH was born in New Hampshire in 1925. His poems have appeared in *Furioso, The New Yorker, The Hudson Review, Poetry Quarterly* (London) , *Harper's Bazaar,* and other magazines. His present residence is at Hanover, N. H.

⫸⫸⫸-⫸⫸⫸-⫸⫸⫸-⫸⫸⫸-⫸⫸⫸-⫸⫸⫸-⫸⫸⫸-⫸⫸⫸-⫸⫸⫷⫷⫷-⫷⫷⫷-⫷⫷⫷-⫷⫷⫷-⫷⫷⫷-⫷⫷⫷-⫷⫷⫷-⫷⫷⫷-⫷⫷⫷

## *Siasconset Song*

The girls
of golden summers whirl
through sunsprung
bright Julys
with born right
sky-bright
star-night
eyes;

everywhere
their tennis twirl
of young gold
legs and arms,
they singsong
summer-long
I-belong
charms;

and through
the summer sailing swirl
they cut like
shining knives
in sun-told
never old
ever gold
lives.

# Cold Water Flat

Come to conquer
this living labyrinth of rock,
young Theseus of Dubuque
finds he is mazed without a minotaur,
without his Ariadne in the dark.

He dreams beyond
his steelwalled fear to fields grown
vertical with corn
and hope. Home to this heroic end:
imprisoned in the city of alone;

here smog obscures
his visionary victor's world,
and streetsounds dulled
with rain reverberate in airshaft hours
where braver conquerors have been felled.

Amazed at night,
stalking the seven maids no sword
can save, he is devoured
in passageways of reinforced concrete,
trapped by his beast, and overpowered

in sleepless dead-
end dreams. How now Theseus? How send
word home you are confined
with neither wings nor lover's thread
in the city that a murderer designed?

G. A. BORGESE was born near Palermo, Sicily, in 1882. He was educated at the University of Milan and taught there. Head of Italy's press and propaganda bureau under Premier Orlando, he refused to take the Fascist oath with the rise of that regime, left for the United States and became an American citizen, teaching for several years at the University of Chicago. His principal books published in America are *The City of Man, Goliath, The March of Fascism,* and *Common Cause.* Magazines in which his work has appeared include *The Nation,* the *Saturday Review,* the *Atlantic Monthly, Life,* and *The American Scholar.* Professor Borgese died at Fiesole in December of 1952.

*Easter Sunday, 1945*

O Sicilia, o Toscana, ove sostai
fanciullo, o dolce pian di Lombardia,
misurato dai gelsi, ventilato
dalle piume dei pioppi, io dunque più
non premerò le vostre vie, levando
il ciglio ai borghi bruni in cima ai
    olivi,
ai fidi vespri reduce cercando
le tue guglie marmoree, Milano
che il respire dei paschi inteneriva
di volubile nube; non più:

 (O Sicily, O Tuscany, where I
In boyhood paused, O sweet
    Lombardy plain,
Measured by mulberry-trees, fanned
    by the feathers
Of poplars, where no more I tread
    your ways,
Lifting my eyes to townships brown
    along

Your hills, or, coming home to
    trusty evenings,
Seeking the marble pinnacles of
    Milan,
Made softer by the breathing of
    the meadows
Where the cloud lingered. Now
    no more.)

                                    dich
nicht, Deutschland, Erde meiner zweiten
    Frühe,
wo klare Ströme rauschten durch
    den dunklen
Duft der sachte weichenden Waldungs-
    nacht,
Geranien aus erwachenden Geländern
mit tausendfält'gen Mädchenlippen
    lachten,
ich aber einsam wandelte von Berg
zu Berg stieg auf ur-rote Glocken-
    türme,
lauschte den Tönen, die die Tiefe
    barg,
die fremde Schöne mit verliebtem
    Auge
fasste: nicht mehr:
                    O Tenebrae! O Aceldama!

                            (Nor thee,
Germany, land of my second prime,
    where the clear streams
Rushed through the fragrant darkness
    of the night,
The slowly yielding woodland night,
    and flowers,
Geraniums, from balconies at morning,
Laughed like a thousand girls, but I
    went, lonely,
Wandered from ridge to ridge, climbing
    bell-towers

Of immemorial red, listened to music
Enclosed in depth, and with my loving
    eyes
Held that strange beauty. Now no more!
O Tenebrae! O Aceldama!)

You passers-by who stop and wonder
what I in uncommuning sounds lament;
it is as if I had left home at noon
and looked homeward before sundown;
    I see
the barns aflame, the house a rump,
    the trees
writhing in desperate embraces; death
with claws of strangling smoke grips
    ground and air.
The silence is one shriek, one chasm
    the paths.
So let me step westward; my shadow
    is long.


## Dream of a Decent Death

### I

Did you deserve a quiet death? did you—
at least since you heard those flutes of the night—
live your life without greed or fear, sloth or
wrath, an unbroken day that earned its sleep?

And did you trust the undisclosed tomorrow?

Then Death will stand by your bedside with folded
wings, ready to receive your last breath, long,
full-drawn, ascendant, like the word expire.

Then dying will be easier much than was
being born, a choice not yours yet willed by
acceptance mild, and there will be no crying,
your name burning past you like a pure lamp.

# II

I dreamed that Death was a staircase of marble,
deep-toned, not black, with fluorescent luster
far-kindled lambent on its massive rails.
I went down step by step and was alone.

I even had asked my young wife to go
to a party where she might hear music and
pass bright drinks on unvacillating trays,
then to report to me late at bedside.

Thus solitary I went the spiral way,
dim but not dark, neither hurrying nor
remiss nor leaning on the stately rails,
self-guided earthward to the large low floor
and bed to lie on and take sober leave.

I thought that everybody in that mansion
lived and died as I did, tuned to the hours,
until he hears the call of his midnight.

CONSTANCE CARRIER was born in New Britain, Conn. Her poems have appeared in the *Atlantic Monthly, Harper's Magazine, Poetry, The Nation,* and *The New Yorker.* A graduate of Smith College, Miss Carrier lives in New Britain, where she is a teacher of Latin in the Senior High School.

>>>->>>->>>->>>->>>->>>->>>->>>->>>-<<<-<<<-<<<-<<<-<<<-<<<-<<<-<<<-<<<-<<<-

## Pro Patria

On a green island in the Main Street traffic
is a granite arch to the dead of the Civil War—
in the Eastlake style, all cubes and tetrahedrons,
each end of the passage barred by an iron-lace
    door.

They are always locked, tho the space between
    is empty—
from door to door it isn't much over a yard:
break open one, you could almost touch the other.
Nobody knows what the locks were meant to
    guard.

East and west, the head of a blank-eyed lion
hisses an arc of spray to the pool below
with a faint persistent sound, an endless whisper,
steady under the traffic's stop-and-go.

On top of the monument stands a gilded lady
casting a wreath forever into space:
her carven robes are decent and concealing:
there is no emotion graven on her face.

Words are cut in the stone above the arches—
THEY JOINED THE MORTAL STRUGGLE
    AND WENT DOWN—
and on every quoin is written the name of a
    battle
that bloodied creek or landing, bluff or town,

now dry and hard in history and granite.
In summer the sun lies hot upon the stone,
and the bums and the drunks and the old men
    and the pigeons
take over the little island for their own.

The old men sit on a bench, with nuts and
    breadcrusts
for the birds to eat from their hands: the
    ne'er-do-wells
sprawl on the grass and drowse and boast and
    argue:
the drunks discourse like statesmen and oracles,

while the birds skim over their heads with a
    cardboard clatter
of wings, or mince on the pavement at their feet . . .
They are all of them tolerant of one another
in this world like a bubble, this island in the street.

The sun is warm, the lions hiss, and the faithful
loaf in their places, lazy and benign,
a little hierarchy who inherit
this plot of earth, this obsolescent shrine.

Who can recall the day of that war's ending?
Think of our own time, then, the summer night
when the word came, and all the churchbells
    sounded
the end of the dark and the coming of the light.

How many times how many towns have seen it,
the light, the hope, the promise after the dark—
seen it, and watched it flicker and ebb and vanish,
leaving no trace except some little park

where no one recalls that dream, that disillusion,
and a monument to death is only known
as a place where the harmless unambitious gather
and the doves come down for bread on the
    sun-warmed stone.

# Peter at Fourteen

What do you care for Caesar, who yourself
are in three parts divided, and must find,
past daydream and rebellion and bravado,
the final shape and substance of your mind?

What are the Belgae, the Helvetii
to you? I doubt that you will read in them
metaphor of your stand against dominion,
or see as yours their desperate stratagem.

They found their tribal rank, their feuds, their
 freedom,
obliterated, lost beyond return.
It took them years to see that law and order
could teach them things that they might care
 to learn.

As fiercely individual, as violent
as they, you clutch your values and your views,
fearful that self may not survive absorption.
(Who said *to learn* at first is like *to lose?*)

Not courage, no, but nature will betray you.
You will stop fighting, finally, and your pride,
that fed so long upon your independence,
flourish on what convention can provide,

till you may grow more Roman than the Romans,
contemptuous of pagan broils and brawls,
and even, mastering your mentors' knowledge,
go on to build cathedrals, like the Gauls.

# Seminary

They go along the graveled walks,
a straggle of academy girls
with notebooks and with hockey sticks—
from blue berets to ankle socks
as much alike as peas or pearls.

Their uniform is their defense
against a too-large world, their claim
to be both separate and the same—
at once distinguished and at once
group-blurred to any casual glance.

Unmindful of the rule's intent,
of what their pious elders meant—
that all mutations of the breed
are equal in the sight of God
and cause for neither shame nor pride—

they do not question such a rule:
it, or its letter, they betray
in the belief that they obey.
They are not rebels, not at all—
only intensely practical.

They recognize their own elect,
discriminate, appraise, condemn,
and, with no hint of disrespect,
almost unconsciously they come
to change *One should be* to *I am.*

THOMAS COLE was born in 1922 in Baltimore, Md. Holder of degrees from Muhlenberg College and the University of Pennsylvania, Mr. Cole has published poems in *Poetry*, *Voices*, *Botteghe Oscure*, and in other magazines from Japan and India to London. Editor of *Imagi*, he lives in Baltimore, where he is occupied with social work for the Department of Public Welfare.

>>>->>>->>>->>>->>>->>>->>>->>>->>>->>>-<<<-<<<-<<<-<<<-<<<-<<<-<<<-<<<-<<<-<<<

## Variations on a Still Morning

Now I see the leaves tilting
There where the wind suddenly is,
Having slowed to stillness most of the
    morning.

Having slowed to silence
For the trees shimmer but do not sound,
Only the sun sings in the foliage.

Having the morning yet slowed,
The birds have forgotten their songs,
Do not dart between the low branches,

Are silent or gone. All is
Silence, all is stillness, all is
Slowed. Leaves are not greenlight

But silver and black. O birds,
Shake your golden cymbals
Amid the leafage of these breathless trees.

## La Grande Jatte: Sunday Afternoon

Seurat looked well to see these people
Leisurely pass their Sunday on the Jatte:
Madame, exact and stiff yet utterly relaxed,
Parades her monkey. Her barely-there escort
Is elegant in his dark suit and top hat,

Cane and cigar. One feels at once the fine
Distortions. The little dog's excited bark
Fails to arouse the interest of the hound.
And the three idlers continue in their mood
Of contemplation. Nothing is stark

Or sudden in this scene, and one recalls,
With an inner smile, darling Degas' objection:
'Too little motion.' Finding the green is not
So green as sunny, the eye is beguiled
Out of proper focus. Here convention

Is flouted and flaunted in true French fashion.
There is coupled with rightness and poise
An innocent nonchalance in just proportions.
See how the girls amid their folded skirts
Hear but ignore the raucous noise

Of ducks. And there by the shore a lady's
Intent on fishing. Above her head white sails turn
In the breeze, the only sign of boundless energy.
The isle is full of noises, sounds, and airs;
Movement is the theme, yet all is still. To learn

The secrets of this atmosphere, I spend
The hour: before my eye the sun contracts
And grows where motion is. And here
In this sunlit shade beyond the frame
I note with what calm grace the French relax.


## 'My Lady Takes the Sunlight for Her Gown'

My lady takes the sunlight for her gown,
Won't burn with it; she has an inner fire
Of her own. Still in the morning sun she sings,
Then sighs and threads an antique tapestry.

The burning in her eye doth shame the sun,
Recalls the white light of a recent fire
Whenas I played the shuttle to her loom,
That rack of bliss unto our coupled pain.

There is no stirring from her threading now.
She would unweave the fabric of that night,
Unravel as it were our ravelings,
And weave them on her loom for future nights.

See how the sunlight weaves her memory!
She sings and threads her antique tapestry.

## The Landscape of Love

Waking with morning, I note the empty
Sea. No sail ventures on

That calm. And there she stands against
The sun, brushing her golden hair

By the open window, while I must time
Such beauty so the moments stay

Locked in the brightest corner of
The mind. She laughs (part of the game)

"Count on. The sun is blind. The moon,
"That fickle fellow of the night,

"Fades in my light." I think of a stretch
Of beach sprung with disturbing thistle

Holding back the affirming sea.
Here by the window her light taunts

That old lover the Sun. Sun,
Do not deny her goldenness, for in

The night (though she burn), she
Is all of darkness in the dark.

# The Tray

In a week of perpetual rain
The ragged mind goes picking
For past summers among
The cluttered attic galleries:

Apprehended on a white petal,
Its pressed wings poised
For the air, the butterfly
Has alighted for ever.  Nothing
Detains those amber fans
From their impending flight.
The roses open or are about
To open, the mind dizzy
With their stopped perfume.
Caught in the filaments of blown
Milkweed, the bee in its golden armor,
Always about to take
The rose, grows keen merely
Awaiting that touch of greatness
Held in the balance.  And not yet
Drunk with fulfillment, it staggers
Never homeward through no dark
Alleyways, hiding its happiness.

What woods what fields what lawns
What lone artificer
Gave up these summer joys
To make this tray?  that now
In company of boots, oil lamps,
Hoops, and ribboned packets
Of letters holds a season
Constant, green and perfect.

PADRAIC COLUM was born in Ireland in 1881. He is a member of the Academy of Irish Letters as well as of the American Institute of Arts and Letters. His publications include *Collected Poems,* and numerous other items. Mr. Colum lives in New York City.

━━━━━━━━━━━━━━━━━━━━━━━━━━

## *At Ferns Castle*

Here, as a bare, unlichened wall, the Castle front
   goes up,
And empty inside, empty all, as empty as a cup
A laggard left within the breach after the last sup.

But horses glistened in the court, the breed of
   Saladin,
And falcons from MacMurrough's perch looked
   round with baleful eyne;
The Statutes of FitzEmpress were held by aureate
   men.

I look to where the apertures, one over one, make
   space
Within the massiveness of wall: Such blue there
   never was!
Never in any place, I say, was such translucent glass!

And then the thought: how ignorant! No window-
   pane was set
Within the depth of loop-hole that I am gazing at,
Making scrutable the figured cloth where prancing
   beast meets scathe.

And thereupon entrancement grew: clear and
   unearthly
As syllables in holy words the blue was lined on
   high:
At Ferns Castle yesterday I looked upon the sky!

# On Not Hearing the Birds Sing
## in Ireland

The Blackbird of Litir Lone
That pensive Finn famed so,
The thrush that in the evening sang
*Air baun chnuic Eireann—o*

Where have they gone and left our woods
And fields without a note
Except the ground tone of the rooks
Gathered from their rout?

The simple fields now make their own
Of the unusèd light;
More than the hedge, the ivy crop
On ruined wall is bright;

And now the grass-tufts take the glow,
The thorn bush is revealed
A relic of the ancientry
The rath has left the field;

And Katie on her doorstep stands
Withheld; she would call in
The errant clutch the yellow hen
Has hatched out in the whin.

But no bird sings from thorn bush,
From hedge or leafy sill—
Where have they gone, the speckled breast,
And where, the yellow bill?

What grim marauder made a spoil
Of bird and nestling,
And left to us the songless woods,
The songless fields of Eirinn?

## Olive Trees

With caverned bole and twisted limb they bide,
Of their grained branches sparing, as old age
Is sparing of the rankness that's in youth—
    These Olive Trees.

They have the greyness of dim mornings when
Noah or Numa walked the hillside; they
Fall less into decay than into ruin—
    These stone-grey Trees.

And are of man's domain as oxen are—
Therefore more ancient than the forest trees,
As ancient as his walls or as his ships—
    These labored Trees.

## Catalpa Tree

Catalpa tree with trunk like monolith,
Wide-reaching branches and a thick of leaves
As green as is lush grass
As wide as open hands.

And we remember how your blossoms came
Amid the freshness of your large green
    leaves—
Whiter than seagulls' breasts,
A thousand thousand blooms.

And like men of good heart who proffer all,
Descending branches held out boons to us—
Branches of blossoms rare,
White, freaked and delicate.

Then strewed them on the ground, and
    distances
Being native to these trees, strewed them
    so deep
For prairie winds to strew
Across unbounded lands.

And like a King who waives all less estates
For sovereignty, you stand in greatness now,
Sans duchies of leaves,
Sans baronies of blooms.

## Poplar Tree

And worth the blossoms that acacias
And chestnuts wear are these
Leaves that number and that motion have
And verberation of the wind and rain—
Leaves that ensky themselves; and so,
By Cypress, Olive, Myrtle shown to be
       Child of the Celtic lands,
With furrowed bole and black the Poplar stands.

## Dahlias

    When we behold
Flowers of the magnitude of these,
We dream the gardens that were Atlas's
Before the pride of his descendants made
Atlantis but a name.  Dahlias
Beside the nettle-green of Autumn gardens,
      Yellow as masks of gold,
Dark-red like wine the Sea Kings pour from
  galleys,
And pink like clouds the early oarsman
Above bright Ophir and dark Gades sees.

## Lilies

    At the White Mass
    The word's not said
    That consecrates;
    The bread stays bread,
    The wine is wine. . . .
    These Lilies hold

As for that rite
Their chalices:
The Mass is white.
But they are garnished
As for that miracle
That turns the natural
Into supernal.


## Belfast: High Street

The City clocks point out the hours—
They look like moons on the darkened towers.

And I who was shown my destination
Thrice, but have no sense of location,

Am back again where one or another
Looming clock has changed a figure.

Moments a thousand have hurried over:
From the sought place I'm as far as ever.

The City clocks point out the hours—
They look like moons on the darkened towers.

That Time and Place are a tangled skein
Their mingled strokes tell over again.


## Dublin: The Old Squares

As I went down through Dublin City
At the hour of twelve of the night,
Who did I see but a Spanish lady
Washing her feet by candle light.
First she washed them,
Then she dried them,
All by a fire of amber coals,
In all my life I never did see
A maid so neat about the soles.

I asked her would she come a-walking,
And we went on where the small bats flew;
A coach I called then to instate her,
And on we drove till the grey cocks crew.
        Combs of amber
        In her hair were,
        And her eyes had every spell.
In all my life I never did see
A maid whom I could love so well.

But when I came to where I found her,
And set her down from the halted coach,
Who was there waiting, his arms folded,
But that fatal swordsman, Tiger Roach?
        Then blades were out,
        And 'twas thrust and cut,
        And never wrist gave me more affright,
Till I lay low upon the floor
Where she stood holding the candle light.

But, O ye bucks of Dublin City,
If I should see at twelve of the night
In any chamber, such lovely lady
Washing her feet by candle light,
        And drying o'er
        Soles neat as hers,
        All by a fire of amber coal—
Your blades be dimmed! I'd whisper her,
And take her for a midnight stroll!

J. V. CUNNINGHAM was born in Cumberland, Md., in 1911. His books of poetry include *The Helmsman, The Judge is Fury* and *Doctor Drink;* he has also written a critical study: *Woe or Wonder: The Emotional Effect of Shakespearean Tragedy.* Mr. Cunningham lives in Charlottesville, Va., where he is Assistant Professor of English at the University of Virginia.

-->>>-->>>-->>>-->>>-->>>-->>>-->>>-->>>-->>>-->>>-->>><<<--<<<--<<<--<<<--<<<--<<<--<<<--<<<--<<<--<<<--<<<--

# *Epigrams*

**1.**
Here lies my wife. Eternal peace
Be to us both with her decease.

**2.**
The Elders at their services begin
With paper offerings. They release from sin
The catechumens on the couches lying
In visions, testimonies, prophesying:
Not, "Are you saved?" they ask, but in informal
Insistent query, "Brother, are you normal?"

**3.**
*Arms and the man I sing,* and sing for joy,
Who was last year all elbows and a boy.

**4.**
I had gone broke, and got set to come back,
And lost, on a hot day and a fast track,
On a long shot at long odds, a black mare
By Hatred out of Envy by Despair.

**5.**
You wonder why *Drab* sells her love for gold?
To have the means to buy it when she's old.

**6.**
The man who goes for Christian resignation
Will find his attitude his occupation.

**7.**
You ask me how Contempt who claims to sleep
With every woman that has ever been
Can still maintain that women are skin deep?
They never let him any deeper in.

**8.**
Friend, on this scaffold Thomas More lies dead
Who would not cut the Body from the Head.

**9.**
And what is love? Misunderstanding, pain,
Delusion, or retreat? It is in truth
Like an old brandy after a long rain,
Distinguished, and familiar, and aloof.


## *Horoscope*


Out of my birth
The magi chart my worth;
They mark the influence
Of hour and day; they weigh what thence

Will come to me.
I in their cold sky see
No Venus and no Mars:
It is the past that cast the stars

That guide me now.
In winter, when the bough
Has lost its leaves, the storm
That piled them deep will keep them warm.

BABETTE DEUTSCH (Mrs. Avrahm Yarmolinsky) was born in New York City in 1895. Miss Deutsch is the author of six volumes of poetry, of which the most recent is *Take Them, Stranger;* another is in preparation. She has also written books of criticism, the latest being *Poetry in Our Time,* as well as fiction and juveniles, and has translated the work of Pushkin, Rilke, and other poets. She has won several awards, and holds an honorary Litt. D. from Columbia University, where she is guest professor of English. Her home is in New York City.

## New Words for an Old Song

Few hours remain. Darkness is big, is surly,
And will not let departure wait;
While Hardy's song in the going's hurly-burly
Truly declares: "If grief comes early,
    Joy comes late."

Oh, there is joy: the heart, as if it were snowing
Pleasure's feathers, is tattooed with light.
And eyes, even in hatchings framed, are glowing
Fire-new. What if a cold wind's blowing
    Back of the night?

But darkness does not pause, is moving nearer
To claim the small familiar weight
Of a wrinkled sack of pains. The end grows clearer,
What's left more sharply sweet, dearer and dearer.
    Joy comes late.

## Reflections in a Little Park

On dusty benches in the park
I see them sit from noon till dark,
Infirm and dull, or glum and dry,
And think, as I go stepping by:

"There—but for the grace of God—sit I!"
Yet cannot blink and cannot bless
God's manifest ungraciousness.


## Piano Recital

FOR MARO AJEMIAN AND JOHN CAGE

Her drooping wrist, her arm
Move as a swan should move,
First singing when death dawns
Upon the plumaged flesh.
But here no swan wings thresh,
No river runs. A woman
Strikes hidden strings in love.

Now slow—as fronds of palms—
Her fingers on the keys.
Lifted, her listening arms
Ponder the theme afresh,
Until it seems young flesh
Is momently transmuted
To echo's effigy.

No no—the risen hands
Pounce on the keys, destroy
The hush, rush on, command
The blacks, the ivories,
In flight now with the keys
To grief's unwindowed prison,
To the low gate of joy.

She leans with sparkling looks
Toward the dark wood, her strong
Hands work as gleaners should.
Then, as who would caress
A birdlike wordlessness,
She stoops—to drink the meaning
At the still brink of song.

# They Came to the Wedding

Like gods who are fêted,
Like friendly old slaves,
Their silence full of music,
Their hands full of flowers,
Singly, in waves,
They came to the wedding.

First, sceptered with sunlight,
Slicing the shadows,
The Pharaoh came decked
In power, in sereneness
Like that of the lotus,
The lively, erect
Flower of forever.

The empress of China
Paraded her dragons
Of silver and gold,
While mountains were unloosing
Their hair to the music
Waterfalls trolled
Like bells for the wedding.

Saints came and sailors
With stories of marvels
And marvelous gifts,
And masts that now were branches
Broke into bird-song
Floating in drifts
Down branching horizons.

The deserts danced after,
The rivers before,
Till darkness like a mortal
Denying immortals
Thrust from the door
Those who came for the wedding.

LEAH BODINE DRAKE was born in Chanute, Kans., in 1914, grew up in Lexington, Ky., and now lives in Evansville, Ind. She has published one book, *A Hornbook for Witches*, and her poems have appeared often in *Poetry*, *Saturday Review*, *Voices*, The *Atlantic Monthly*, *The New Yorker*, and elsewhere. In 1950 Miss Drake won the second prize in the annual contest of the Poetry Society of America, and this year won first prize given by *Poetry Awards* for her poem *Precarious Ground*.

## The Final Green

This is of green—unclassic shade
Of which the Greek tongue was afraid,
Symbol of the distance, where
Pure form melts into formless air,
A Saracenic color, green,
From lands beyond the Byzantine—
Soul of the emerald, the dye
Of Persian tile and tiger's eye,
Of mermaid's hair and peacock's tail,
The Prophet's flag, the Holy Grail.

Green, the moon's proverbial cheese,
The blood within the veins of trees,
The famous hue of envy's face,
Our planet's little light in space:
Earth's color, where her peoples pass
Under the final green of grass.

# Honey from the Lion

I came upon it unaware. . . .
First there was sand and silence there,
Blue-burning haze and scorching rock,
Short-daggered grass . . . and then the shock
Of great limbs stretched before a lair:

The old brave body, stiff and prone,
Of some king-lion done to death
Upon the threshold of his earth,
All that huge ardor still as stone.

Wild bees had built their honeycomb
In his bright carcass, thunder-maned.
Through brow and jaw the nectar strained:
What Pharaoh in his spicy tomb
Had such rich amber seal his mouth?

I dipped my fingers in the sweet
And oh! the fiery savage meat
Bred from the lands of lack and drouth,
Tanged with wild joy and deep unrest
And desolate courage and the strength
Of loneliness: I knew at length
What fury burned in Samson's breast!

Now garden honey's overmild
To satisfy the sharpened taste
Of one who's eaten of the Waste.
I know a hunger never filled
Since that strange banquet long ago,
That dark and bitter sweetness grown
Out of the lion's blood and bone,
Out of the desert's pride and woe.

LORA DUNETZ, who was born in New York City, is on
military leave from The University of Maryland Hospital,
where she served as Director of Occupational Therapy; and
is now a First Lieutenant with the Women's Medical Specialist
Corps. Her poems have appeared in *Furioso, Imagi, Experiment, Epos, Kaleidograph.*

->>>->>>->>>->>>->>>->>>->>>->>>->>>->>><<<-<<<-<<<-<<<-<<<-<<<-<<<-<<<-<<<-<<<-

# *"and all the while the sky is falling ..."*
### FOR THOMAS COLE

It is late afternoon at the beach; I lie on the swaying dock,
One arm overhanging the edge and my hand
Playing with the muddy water of the Chesapeake,
And I am wondering what it is that is wrong with the
    world and with mankind;

And other trite thoughts invade my mind as the tide
    recedes . . .
The tawny children abandon the rocks and the yellow
    rafts,
And the wind through the mouth of a half-empty beer
    bottle broods
Like a lonely faraway foghorn, in rhythmic drifts

Taking the shape of words whose name might be **fear**
    perhaps,
Or a sort of resignation, or protest, or bitterness
Rising from a sigh at the heart and a curl to the lips,
That this so permanent beautiful sky, alas,

Should fall, on this so beautiful ailing earth, as it was
    written
In the first book I ever read (and how we laughed!)
*Oh, Henny Penny, look! the sky is falling!*
    And now the rotten-
ness becomes apparent in the brittle weft

And the whole cloth crumbles like old wood-pulp paper
That feels like death in your fingers, and is hardly worth
    bothering

51

About. And, as so-and-so said once, when I was only
  half there,
It might as well be smoke and ashes—it isn't worth a
  farthing.

## While the Bells Ring

Pursuer, eluder
Lying in wait at the snare or evading the trap
Afraid of the sharp, the sudden, the accidental,
Man, the great carnivore, daily on the hunt
In the forest or market-place for the not-fleet-enough
Sits in the semishade of his veranda on Sunday
Comforted by the second warmth of coffee
At peace with his world, his house, his Self
And turns from an editorial presaging the doom of
                    the species
To Superman,
While the bells ring praises.

## Treason

The surrounding woods are burning with subdued
  fire,
the rusty chrysanthemums betray the smolder

of summer's ash; the sky sweeps over the land
in autumn's consummate blue and white. The burnt

and brittle leaves drift through the shining air
crackling to nature's harvest, and the careful listener

can hear the grass leap to its final fraction
on the stem; the fruit on the trees hangs taut as wax,
  and

full of reward. Symbols of peace and plenty
enrich the abounding day. And who knows why

a hungry hawk that catches October's lights
as it tips a static wing in the exploits

of survival—and, truly, meaning no harm—
should suddenly see a chicken devouring a worm. . . .

RICHARD EBERHART was born in Austin, Minn., in 1904. His books of poetry include *Burr Oaks* and *Undercliff,* the latter to be published this year. Mr. Eberhart has won the Shelley Memorial Award, and served as a judge on the Bollingen Prize Award committee at the Yale University Library. His permanent residence is in Cambridge, Mass.; he has spent the past year as Visiting Professor of English at the University of Washington in Seattle.

## The Human Being Is a Lonely Creature

It is borne in upon me that pain
Is essential. The bones refuse to act.
Recalcitrancy is life's fine flower.
The human being is a lonely creature.

Fear is of the essence. You do not fear?
I say you lie. Fear is the truth of time.
If it is not now, it will come hereafter.
Death is waiting for the human creature.

Praise to harmony, to love.
They are best, all else is false.
Yet even in love and harmony
The human being is a lonely creature.

The old sloughed off, the new newborn,
What fate and what high hazards join
As life tires out the soul's enterprise.
Time is waiting for the human creature.

Life is daring all our human stature.
Death looks, and waits for each bright eye.
Love and harmony are our best nurture.
The human being is a lonely creature.

53

# Sainte Anne de Beaupré

The sun saw on that widening shore
Three hundred mothers with their daughters.
All dressed in white they followed slowly
Their mothers to the great stone doors.

O Bonne Sainte Anne
O Bonne Sainte Anne
The priest intoned upon the electric air.

The wind was bright from hundred years
And bright from off that distant shore
As slowly walked the maidens with
Their mothers to the cold church door.

A spectacle of heavenly imagery
And sun and wind upon the place,
The slow procession seemed a dream of time
While loudly through the air the cry implored

O Bonne Sainte Anne
O Bonne Sainte Anne,
Protectress of these children in their time.

Bronze on the hill, beyond the heavy Church
Stood dark the Stations of the Cross
In groves deep hidden from the sight
And from the brightness of such angelance.

O Bonne Sainte Anne,
O Bonne Sainte Anne,
Loudspoken tone upon white-flowing air.

Three hundred maidens beside their mothers
Slowly mount the tributary steps,
Entering to receive the blessing
Thought beyond all human ill.

O Bonne Sainte Anne!
O Bonne Sainte Anne!
An ancient spell lifts high in air!

And slowly came at last with blessings
And slowly down the prospect walked
And formed a slow and long procession
Of sun and wind and timeless innocence.

O Bonne Sainte Anne,
O Bonne Sainte Anne,
Protect the young in their extremity,
The wish of men who know all evil.

Such ecstasy had filled the hearts of many
And made so glad the light of tender eyes
It is a hurt that dream is not eternity,
And Bonne Sainte Anne not hunted down
   by time.

## Ur Burial

Reach me a blue pencil of the moon,
The double-reined rings from tombs of Ur,
The lyre, the javelins from Sumer,
"The Ram caught in a thicket."

A gold dagger, a golden toilet case,
The gold helmet of Meskalam-dug;
Rein-ring and mascot from
Queen Shub-ad's chariot.

I will drink a narcotic rich and dark.
I will lie down by my master in his sarcophagus,
All our company will join in sleep
To serve the sun in a life beyond sleep.

## The Horse Chestnut Tree

Boys in sporadic but tenacious droves
Come with sticks, as certainly as Autumn,
To assault the great horse chestnut tree.

There is a law governs their lawlessness.
Desire is in them for a shining amulet
And the best are those that are highest up.

They will not pick them easily from the ground.
With shrill arms they fling to the higher branches,
To hurry the work of nature for their pleasure.

I have seen them trooping down the street
Their pockets stuffed with chestnuts shucked,
    unshucked.
It is only evening keeps them from their wish.

Sometimes I run out in a kind of rage
To chase the boys away; I catch an arm,
Maybe, and laugh to think of being the lawgiver.

I was once such a young sprout myself
And fingered in my pocket the prize and trophy.
But still I moralize upon the day

And see that we, outlaws on God's property,
Fling out imagination beyond the skies
Wishing a tangible good from the unknown.

And likewise death will drive us from the scene
With the great flowering world unbroken yet,
Which we held in idea, a little handful.

ABBIE HUSTON EVANS was born in Lee, N. H., in 1881. She has published two books of poems, *Outcrop,* and *The Bright North.* Winner of the Guarantors' Prize given by *Poetry,* Miss Evans is on the advisory board of *Contemporary Poetry.* She lives in Philadelphia.

‹‹‹‹‹‹‹‹‹‹‹‹‹‹‹‹‹‹‹‹‹‹‹‹‹‹‹‹‹‹‹‹‹

## By the Salt Margin

### *(In Time of Uncertainty)*

By the salt margin where life first broke cover
The reek of seaweed bids the blood remember.
Struck through with sun, incorporate with ledge,
Like a pelt stretched on a door for the sun to cure,
I now attest existence. Heat pours down
Like rain upon me, drenching the lichened ledge,
The chained-down limpet and the forspent body.

Now side and hand and foot-sole have to do
The thinking for me. Tell me not "about,"
Deliver the thing itself, its sting or nothing.
O unworn senses, mint the minutes sharp,
Make each one be a gold-piece. Being is all.
I know at last firsthand as Moses did
Jehovah's final name is deep I AM.

## This World

Early and late the backdrop is for joy;
The makings of wonder hang up on the air.
Fine, fine, like something seen from under the
    hand
On a morning in autumn, early, waits this world.

The heart sings out to see it hanging there
Half-apparition, marks it for its own,
Accepts the marvel freely as a child
That bends above the fadeless rock with laughter.

The forestage is the trouble; man made that,
And cannot blame another. (This I knew,
Returning to the changeless purpled mountain.)
Inept, impatient, like a fractious child

He tangles ropes and cords into a knot
That all but stops the play. Yet all the while
The makings of wonder hang up on the air,
Early and late the backdrop is for joy.

## Come to Birth

All lesser reasons for loving die away
Before this one: that you had power to make
Demand on me which I had power to meet;
That you could make demand so deep that I
Could meet it only by an act of birth,
Watching creation like a looker-on,
Myself the thing created out of dust.
Well may I own the power that does this thing.
With shaken breath I fear to look on the face
Of this great-statured self that bowed in the dark.
Decision now out of my hand is torn
And passes to this other at its birth,
And what shall happen I no longer know.

## Euroclydon

The east-northeaster pounds the coast tonight,
Thudding and grinding at the knees of islands;
It sets the bell-buoys clanging and calls out
The gruff storm-warnings up and down the coast.

—So this, none else, was Paul's Euroclydon,
That old tempestuous wind that leaped from Crete
And heaped the seas up till they broke the ship,
But not the man. —Pull out the Book again:
"When the south wind blew softly—" (O sweet
    words,
The spring is in them. Hark!) — "we loosed from
    Crete."

I sit and listen while Euroclydon,
That old storm-wind that had a name of its own
Two thousand years before I yet had mine,
Pelts on my pane with blizzard snow like grit,
Shrieks down my chimney, grips my house
    foursquare,
And pants against my door.
               *Old tiger, hail!*

# Return to Life

The southwest wind blows in from the sea unceasing,
The brown hawk falls in the field. Once more I live.
Like a hand pulled free from a glove I finger edges,
Ease and expand like a dry sponge drinking water.
Now like a too-tight cord that can untwist
Its tortured length, and spinning round and round
Resign old tension back into the air,
I am escaped from the thumb and finger of life.
Shaken loose like a tassel at last, I hang, I swing;
A breath can whiff me round, this way or that.

While the robin calls with his colored note for rain
And the bright cattle watch me from the pasture,
The cranberry's cold little apples deep in the marsh
Feel good to my hand that goes groping, sun beats on
    my shoulder,
Heat flatters my cheek, pouring up from the floor of
    the meadow.
Seeing the boxberry plums hid under the leaves,

And this year's arbutus plants, crisped, hugging the bank,
And the lady's-slipper leaves, paired, wedged in the mold,
I dally along at my ease, keeping step with the sun.
I make free with myself at last; I see that we are friends.


## Sun-up in March

No wonder the birds make whittlings of sound, that
    the hemlock
Prepares to dip and plume in the wind, dead-sure
Of what is now on the way from the edge of the
    world.

That blazing bale in the thicket is bright day
Upbundled, fubbed in a ball; conglomerate glory
Inrolled, constricted to one nub of fire.
See how a whole day rages, telescoped
On itself, foreshortened to a furnace-blaze
Behind the wattle of the alder swamp.
—Or has earth's floor turned into sky's sea-bottom
Harboring treasure undredged, a crown-jewel heap
That pooling time's splendor and glitter unwavering
    burns?

What underbrush can hide a thing like day,
Or hope to hold it with so frail a lattice?
Yet in a snare as it were the great bird of day
Nests for a moment of time on the floor of the
    swamp.
Presently rising over the rim of the world
It will be on us unmasked; but now for a little
The creature's eye looks level into day's
And sees time end-on burning.
                    —If a day
Can blind like this, what of a year? Oh what
Of a century at one glance? What of that fury?

ANNEMARIE EWING (Mrs. John H. Towner) was born in Pittsburgh, Pa., in 1910. She is the author of a novel, *Little Gate,* and of short stories published in *Ladies' Home Journal, Seventeen,* and The *Saturday Evening Post,* and has contributed articles to *The New Yorker, Downbeat,* and *Radio Mirror.* Miss Ewing lives in San Pedro, Calif.

---

## Rhyme from Grandma Goose

> This little talent goes to market,
> This little talent goes to pot;
> This little talent feeds on blood as cold
>     as steel,
> This little talent feeds on hot;
> This little talent is for white men,
> This little talent is not:
> Hey diddle diddle too ra loo ra nonny o—
> What kind of talent have you got?
>
> This little talent makes a living,
> This little talent makes a lot;
> This little talent it is possible to steal,
> This little talent can be bought;
> This little talent is for women,
> This little talent is not:
> Sing a song of sixpence and ring a rosy
>     round—
> What kind of talent have you got?
>
> This little talent takes a beating,
> This little talent never fought;
> This little talent wants a sanctimonious heel,
> This little talent wants a sot;
> This little talent for a monster,
> This little talent for a tot:
> Ransom a tansom a turmity and yo heave ho—
> What kind of talent have you got?

# Ballad

Mother mine, Mother mine, what do you see?
What do you see when you look at me?
    I see my ambitions all trampled and torn
    By a daughter who won't be a lady born.

Mother mine, Mother mine, were I a son,
What would you see if I were a son?
    I'd see the tempter, the masculine hex,
    The inescapable threat of sex.

Mother mine, Mother, is that why you stare
At the poor man in greasy overalls there?
    Man? I see Misery, poverty's clerk,
    Coming home dirty each night from work.

Mother mine, Mother, be yet more clear:
Describe more exactly this good woman here.
    Woman? What woman? I see a nice house,
    Obedient children, comformable spouse;
    God Bless Our Security clearly their motto:
    They behave as the nice woman thinks that they
        ought to.

Mother mine, dam us—but don't think to sire us
As well, with this virus a-lodge in your iris.
Neither moteless nor beamless, but sightless the eye
That sees things and not people. Dear Mother,
    good-bye. . . .


# Sleep, Madame, Sleep

*Lullaby for Chorus, Snare Drum, and Wire Whisk*

I was a woman    always liked spangles
Solid gold doodads    and diamond bangles.
Never was cheap.    I was too refined to.
But let a guy make presents    if he'd a mind to.
Some memento    of a cozy little dinner. . . .

Like the registration papers      on a Preakness
      winner.
Didn't do business      with the Man in the Street;
Oil man, cattle man      that was my meat.
Got houses of my own . . .      and money in the bank,
With nobody but      myself to thank.
Never was thrown by      romantic gilding.
What's a Dream Prince got      that an office
      building—
In a good location,      say a mid-town block,
With the leases in your safe      deposit box—
      hasn't got?
Why buy a Prince      when champagne's so cheap?
Only trouble was I never      got much sleep.

Started out early;      born entertainer.
Kicked out my Mom      and got me a trainer.
Had to do something      or die of boredom.
What I did      in the cradle floored 'em.
Made my debut      strip teasing a diaper.
What a fool, Eve,      to let the viper
Talk her *into* clothes      when it's taking 'em off,
As everyone knows,      gets the gilt-edged boff.
Gets the jack and the dough      from the sucker-
      peasants.
So, be it known to all men      by these presents—
These garlands of Steel shares      Preferred, U.S. . . .
These nosegays of mortgages,      added to which
Is this perfume, aroma de      oil well or two—
That it's Early to Bed and      Quick to Undress
Makes a girl solvent,      wealthy, and rich.
Makes a girl also      sometimes weep
In the dead of the night      when she's dead for
      sleep.
Plenty of time to      sleep when you're dead.
Anyhow that's what      I always said.

Wound up loaded      in a creamy satin bed.
Fath-dressed body      Antoine-coiffed head.
Flowers by truck loads,      tapers by dozens.
Tears by two harpies      claimed to be cousins.

Soft organ music    on the loud-speaker.
Faces of sleek-faced    attorneys grow sleeker.
"Whereas deceased . . ."    Harpy lights candle.
Murmurs, "A good girl.    Bit hard to handle
Was all." Other harpy    agrees like a shot.
"We're all the fam'ly    the poor soul's got."
Attorney continues:    "Whereas deceased,
Though rich as sin,    was constantly fleeced
Of something money    can not buy:
To wit and namely:    Sleep. Shut-eye.
Kind of occupational    disease, let's say.
Chronic *maladie*    *de métier.*
Deceased, therefore—    *sic transit omnia*—
Bequeathes her all    to fight insomnia.
Sets up Foundation    that nothing lacks
To aid her fellow    insomniacs."
Harpies goggle-eyed.    "You mean we ain't
To get one cent?"    Harpies faint.

Hear me chuckle.    My old veins,
Recently drained    of aches and pains,
Are filled with something—    ask the mortician—
Keeps me in a cool    soporific condition.
Hands folded peacefully    on my chest,
Alone in my creamy    satin nest,
Now I lay me    down so still.
Nothing to do but    sleep—and I will.
I pray the Lord    my soul to keep . . .
Or take . . . or something    equally deep.
If I should wake    before too long—
No, wait a minute.    I've got that wrong.
So I'm waiting . . . I'm waiting . . .    I'm counting
    sheep.
Seven hundred . . . eight hundred . . . nine . . .
    one grand.
What's going on here?    I don't understand.
I'm up to a million . . .    This I won't stand!
Dear little goldywool    diamond-eyed sheep,
STOP! Lemme outa here!    I *still* can't sleep!

ROBERT FRANCIS was born in Upland, Pa., in 1901. His books of poetry include *Stand with Me Here, Valhalla and Other Poems, The Sound I Listened For,* and *The Face Against the Glass.* He has also written a short novel, *We Fly Away.* Mr. Francis has held a fellowship at the Bread Loaf Writers' Conference, received the Shelley Memorial Award, and the Golden Rose of the New England Poetry Club. He lives at Fort Juniper, Amherst, Mass.

## High Diver

How deep is his duplicity who in a flash
Passes from resting bird to flying bird to fish,

Who momentarily is sculpture, then all motion,
Speed and splash, then climbs again to contemplation.

He is the archer who himself is bow and arrow.
He is the upper-under-world-commuting hero.

His downward going has the air of sacrifice
To some dark seaweed-bearded seagod face to face.

Or goddess. Rippling and responsive lies the water
For him to contemplate, then powerfully to enter.

## Swimmer

I

Observe how he negotiates his way
With trust and the least violence, making
The stranger friend, the enemy ally.
The depth that could destroy gently supports him.
With water he defends himself from water.
Danger he leans on, rests in. The drowning sea
Is all he has between himself and drowning.

65

What lover every lay more mutually
With his beloved, his always-reaching arms
Stroking in smooth and powerful caresses?
Some drown in love as in dark water, and some
By love are strongly held as the green sea
Now holds the swimmer. Indolently he turns
To float. —The swimmer floats, the lover sleeps.


## Pitcher

His art is eccentricity, his aim
How not to hit the mark he seems to aim at,

His passion how to avoid the obvious,
His technique how to vary the avoidance.

The others throw to be comprehended. He
Throws to be a moment misunderstood.

Yet not too much. Not errant, arrant, wild,
But every seeming aberration willed.

Not to, yet still, still to communicate
Making the batter understand too late.


## Beyond Biology

Teased and titillated by the need
Always of something more than necessary,
Some by-product beyond biology,
The poet is like a boy poised on a rock
Who must produce an original waterfall,
Father a brook, or fertilize a tree.
Remember how young Gulliver quenched the fire?
Pure boy. Pure poet. The Lilliputian palace
Was saved, the emperor grateful, but the empress
(How like an empress) was implacably shocked.

# Picasso and Matisse

At Vallauris and Vence, Picasso and Matisse,
A trifling eighteen miles apart,
Each with his chapel, one to God and one to Peace,
Artfully pursue their art.

What seems, not always is, what is, not always seems,
Not always what is so is such.
The Party and the Church at absolute extremes
Are nearly near enough to touch.

At Vallauris and Vence, Picasso and Matisse,
One old, one older than before,
Each with his chapel, one to God and one to Peace,
Peacefully pursue their war.

# Apple Peeler

Why the unbroken spiral, Virtuoso,
Like a trick sonnet in one long, versatile
    sentence?

Is it a pastime merely, this perfection,
For an old man, sharp knife, long night,
    long winter?

Or do your careful fingers move at the stir
Of unadmitted immemorial magic?

Solitaire. The ticking clock. The apple
Turning, turning as the round earth turns.

WALKER GIBSON was born in Jacksonville, Fla., in 1919, brought up in Albany, N. Y., and educated at Yale. His poems have appeared in The *Atlantic Monthly, Harper's Magazine, The New Republic, The New Yorker, Poetry,* and *Furioso.* Mr. Gibson is Assistant Professor of English at Amherst College. A volume of his poems will be published in 1954 by Indiana University Press.

>>>->>>->>>->>>->>>->>>->>>->>>->>>->>>->>><<<-<<<-<<<-<<<-<<<-<<<-<<<-<<<-<<<-<<<-<<<-

# *In Memory of the Circus Ship* Euzkera, *Wrecked in the Caribbean Sea, 1 September 1948*

The most stupendous show they ever gave
Must have been that *bizarrerie* of wreck;
The lion tamer spoke from a green wave
And lions slithered slowly off the deck.

Amazing. And the high-wire artists fell
(As we'd all hoped, in secret) through no net
And ten miles down, a plunge they must know
    well,
And landed soft, and there they're lying yet.

Then, while the brass band played a lanquid waltz,
The elephant, in pearls and amethysts,
Toppled and turned his ponderous somersaults,
Dismaying some remote geologists.

The tiger followed, and the tiger's mate.
The seals leaped joyful from their brackish tank.
The fortuneteller read the palm of Fate—
Beware of ocean voyages—and sank.

Full fathom five the fattest lady lies,
Among the popcorn and the caged baboons,
And dreams of mermaids' elegant surprise,
To see the bunting and the blue balloons.

## Thaw

In time the snowman always dies,
As even children realize
And do not mourn his sad demise.
In April, when he's long been gone,
And I begin to mow the lawn,
The blades will crack his big black eyes.

## David

Master of metaphor, at three
He's learned the language of mirage—
Sees dump trucks climbing every tree;
The sky, he says, is their garage.

And like a derrick, drops his head;
Contrives his airplane arms like flaps;
Mother and father sleep like dead;
Behind the barn the dead cat naps.

This is no simple world. To him
Man is machine, machine is man,
And the corpse talks, the lilies swim.
Of course, we tell him what we can.

## Allergy

Hay, house-dust, or the fur from cats
Cause this preposterous disease;
The skin erupts in little spots,
The eyes leak tears, the victims sneeze.

Maybe it's only in the mind,
Or glands, or just the time of year.
No specialist has quite explained
Whether it's fur of cats, or fear,

And all we know is that our world,
The very pillow where we sleep,
Is somehow not to be endured—
And this is foolish. Still, we weep.

## Billiards

Late of the jungle, wild and dim,
Sliced from the elephant's ivory limb,
Painted, polished, here these spheres
Rehearse their civilized careers—
Trapped in a geometric toil,
Exhibit impact and recoil
Politely, in a farce of force.
For this, I utter no remorse
But praise the complicated plan
That organizes beast and man
In patterns so superbly styled,
Late of the jungle, dim and wild.

## The Umpire

Everyone knows he's blind as a bat.
Besides, it's tricky to decide,
As ball meets mitt with a loud splat,
Whether it curved an inch outside
Or just an inch the other way
For a called strike. But anyway,
Nobody thinks that just because
Instead he calls that close one Ball,
That that was what it really *was*.
    (The pitcher doesn't agree at all.)

His eyes are weak, his vision's blurred,
He can't tell a strike from a barn door—
And yet we have to take his word:
The pitch that was something else before
    (And that's the mystery no one knows)

Has gotten to be a ball by now,
Or got to be called ball, anyhow.
All this explains why, I suppose,
People like to watch baseball games,
Where Things are not confused with Names.

## Essay in Defense of the Movies

Our nation's movies, foolish, false, erotic,
Embarrass the most blindly patriotic—
For instance me, who (since I cannot end them)
Gather myself together to defend them.
Give praise, then, to the two-gun-totin ham
Who shoots his serial way from jam to jam,
The sagebrush hero with the vacant mug
Preposterously singin to his plug.
Into the backdrop sunset see him ride,
Leavin behind his maid, never a bride,
Lovin the cows he ropes, the ropes he twirls,
A nice American boy, afraid of girls.
And if he is, in fact, crude, dumb, and coarse,
Can't you at least find pleasure in the horse?
    Movies of more sophisticated type
Offer a more expensive brand of tripe,
Where bathing suits and butlers are the rule
And champagne's served beside the swimming
    pool.
How strange that folks so handsome and well-
    dressed,
Inspired by all that scenery of the West
That, reel on reel, the Eastern eye beholds,
Should act, however, like fifteen-year-olds:
Shoot one another (BOING!), chase off in cars,
Make puppy love in corners of plush bars,
And carry on like manic millionaires
In that strange world where no one ever swears!
    I have to grant shortcomings in the art.
What is it, then, so captivates the heart?

Why do we sit there, raising all those calluses,
Hour after hour in fancy movie palaces?
It can't be action, characters, or plot.
It must be: we feel *cozy* in that spot.
The body curls and bends and fits right in;
The knees are tucked up underneath the chin;
There's warmth, there's darkness, just sufficient
    room—
It is, you see, a little like the womb,
Where bags of popcorn effortlessly flow
Umbilically to the embryo.

    Who of us would not rather like to smother
There in the dim rococo, dreaming of Mother?
All praise, then, after all, to Hollywood:
Of all that's sacred, first comes motherhood.

RICHARD GILLMAN was born in Northampton, Mass., in 1929. He has published poems in *Poetry* and The *Saturday Review*. He is at present stationed at Albrook Air Force Base in the Canal Zone, where he is Editor of the Air Force weekly newspaper; his military rating is A 1/C.

## Bones of a French Lady in a Museum

These never knew or had a hint
Of what the senses knew. No mark on one
Of sight of sky, of flower scent.

As mute as white, they were a witness
To the running blood, adrenaline and brain.
Involved, they stayed impersonal no less.

Sensations leaped and flowed and slid,
Roused by a song or young male hand.
Bones went along, as it were, for the ride,

Continued firm, continued holding, all
Without a crack of consequence.
(Chip in the leg was made by a fall.)

Behind the glass with chimpanzees
They hang serenely, propped with steel:
Not her at all, but jointing her, these

Kept her together for sixty years,
Containing the shock of her elements;
Now are not her, but especially hers.

## On a Very Young, Very Dead Soldier

The hole in the head where the bullet
Peeked through reveals like a keyhole
The room of the dance after the laughs
And the lights have gone out.

The gray that one would pay to see in action
Merely is a color and a stuff

73

That bears no evidence of having been
Spectacular beyond all other gifts.

Yet this is the brain which, after all,
Had a hand in the burps as well as the loves
Of his short history; which was dumb
To flowers and insects, but had a genius

For judging a mile and the size, precisely,
Of a woman's bust; knew cars
From top to bottom, inside out,
And never queried how the universe runs.

It wired to him the pleasures he kept private
Of scaling ice across the crusted snow
Late in the night with wind in his face;
Of swimming underwater all alone.

It held the borders of his universe
Narrowed to his county's sweet geography
Of hairpin curves, long stretches of concrete
And hills his Ford ascended in high gear.

Worry of wounds which swam this brain
Stopped for the most part with pimples.
War was a monster flashed on a screen,
Seen between kisses and colored cartoons.

Still an incorrigible patron of luck
Fond of accelerators down-to-the-floor,
He tapped the famous and infamous gray
For love.

Where thoughts an hour ago beat mad
Wires to the speechless tongue are still,
Without a vibrant Hell to send, or a whistle,
Low and awful, at the sudden shift of things.

Life nearest to him now creeps through
The zombie-bodied bugs, whose brains
Are hot with pure intent to make
Delicious homes behind his eyes.

Oh, he would be laughing now, derisive
But sincere, to see them coming,
Grim as frankensteins, the curious look
Of conquerors on their silly, silly faces.

ASHTON GREENE was born in Alexandria, La., in 1921. He received the degree of B.A. from Louisiana State University in 1941, served in the Navy 1941-6, studied thereafter at Princeton and Oxford. He is now in the business of importing and exporting, with offices in New Orleans, but lives in Baton Rouge. Some of his poems have been published in *The Poet's Reed*.

>>>->>>->>>->>>->>>->>>->>>->>>->>>->>>->>>->>><<<-<<<-<<<-<<<-<<<-<<<-<<<-<<<-<<<-<<<-<<<

# The Church of the Sacred Heart

What saintly features do abound in the Vatican Museum
and Church,
They raise the hearts and minds to God, the Giver of all,
What saintly features greet the eye on entering St. Peter's
It is a blessing to see them, to appreciate them, to lock
them in the heart.

No thoughts of paradise enter the mind of worshippers
at S.H.
They go away baffled, they know not why or wherefor,
they are annoyed.
These are features that are subtle, the nuances are
difficult to grasp.
Perhaps, in another age, generations will see, and seeing,
know.

Who is that above the altar so high, it is Christ, the stern
lawgiver,
His curl is deceiving, his eyes are not too forgiving, the
long
Fingers point to Heaven for the Just, Rex is he, and Rex
he always is.
Know not what the artist is depicting, it is his idea and
not others'.

What is that on the wall, it is a tormentor of Christ, he
is wearing
Glasses so that he may see whom he is tormenting, but to
those who

75

Know, such were not worn in this age, coming upon
the scene much later,
We who see this tormentor recognize the inhumanity of
his features.

Thus, all through the Church, the theme runs true, the
artist wants
The people to see through different lenses, namely his
own. Is it
Worth the time to scrutinize, is it worth the while to
appraise,
Will this live through time, we know what vicissitudes
of fate.

This the living must answer, I have no answer, the seeds
of time
Demand Nostradamus and his prophecies. This we can
aver, the ravages
Of Time will not lightly detract from the ideas depicted,
for these
Pictures show us, the living, our true character, living
out of age. . . .

## The Parade

Time is moving, people move up and down,
The tiger is restless, the cool air is still.
Crowds pour into the narrow streets,
All expectant, what do they see?

Here it comes, here it comes. There is
Humpty Dumpty, but where is Mary had a little?
Four floats and here comes Mary. Mary quite
Contrary was there.

The struggling humanity, for a time forget.
The exuberance of the children smother.
Yet, beneath to return to humdrum, to leave
World of make-believe, live as children—the
Parade.

# The Lagoon

Colors in the sun, colors at night, the Army, Navy and
  Marines
Had conspired to bring civilization to the ringed sands.
  Wars
Can maneuver, but can they break, these are the sterile
  lands,
They support little, the waving palm above it soars
  towards the blue.
The blue underneath the ripples, the small and
  the monstrous, the
Denizens of the Ocean and the sea, here and there, swim
  about.

What freak of nature conspired, however, in the first
  place,
To place you here in the wide open seas, you lie
  unprotected,
You are buffeted about by storms, yet you can endure it,
Even become stronger in adversity. What good are you,
  O sterile
Lands, in wars you help, but having won, you are soon
  forgotten.

Torments of night, torments of day, the sun, the wind,
  the stars,
Sweep over, and over sweep, watching, dodging, seeking,
  even
Swaying. Civilization can mean but little, it is our
  interpretation
We are modern, so were the First Century Romans. We
  who are so
Bent on carrying the fruits of our life, forget that we
  too can
Learn, for who of us can ever make a sterile land a
  lagoon?

# A Bather in a Painting

The water is cool, there is a faint smile,
You step here, you step there, but to go farther
You dislike, it is deep, and beyond what creatures
Lurk, it is difficult to say, but you look, you smile
Yet, beyond there is something, something that beckons
What could it be, what could it be, a rose?

The artist conceives, the model stands, there is a certain
Communion of spirit, what it is, what it could be, we
    question.
The bright purity of the skin, the softness of the hair,
Something is there, the artist catches but a fleeting
    glimpse,
But catching it, he fashions it, he molds it for us to gaze upon.
There is no madonna smile, there is no Titian
    voluptuousness,
There is a light of softness, a moment's glimpse, a still
    thought.
Beyond, beyond the thought, beyond the gaze, a lingering
    look.
We ask, we wonder, but to whom do we direct our
    thoughts?
Surely, not to the artist, but to the figure, to the figure
Approaching the water, so kindly, so sweetly, as if
    impelled
By no thought but to please the onlooker. There is no
    thought.
Can this be changed, can this be seen by the photog-
    rapher's eye?
Doubting, doubting, it could be portrayed but by artist
    colors,
That communion that exists between the artist and
    model to depict
Is difficulty itself, where beyond the seashore, where
    beyond the
Faint outlines of a figure dancing on the sands, here
    touched by
Water, here touched by sunshine, here touched by the
    eternal. . . .

78

JOHN HAY was born in Ipswich, Mass., in 1915. An editor during the war, of *Yank,* the army weekly, Mr. Hay has published one book of poems, *A Private History.* He lives on Cape Cod, in the town of Brewster.

>>>->>>->>>->>>->>>->>>->>>->>>->>><<<-<<<-<<<-<<<-<<<-<<<-<<<-<<<-<<<

## Variations on a Theme

### 1

When fury sings like nothing, like a war,
The need is fury.  Blest be the children's rage
In its own fruit. Blest be the warrior ant
In its own hill.  Its desert saps the sun.

### 2

The dust demands its lightning. Let first
    come first.
Dust of an ancient sea bed takes the rain,
And drives its thunder down. Blest be the dust.
The air takes out of it the first to pray.

### 3

As men are of the air, and air is want,
Flowing with fire and rage, listen, be still.
The apples' golden cymbals clash and repeat
The fruitfulness of wind, in hands of air.

### 4

Like war, wrecking past desire, the hurricane,
Unlike a war, is founded in desire.
The heart of wonder is a peaceful one.
In the origins of rage, the child is love.

### 5

Triumphant peace shines like the growing
    leaves,
With stars and molten lava in their veins.
The infinite space that shines to children's feet
Burns in their bones. The world is in their eyes.

**79**

## Natural Architecture

Molded to the owl is what the owl spits out,
As dry cocoons of mice—gray fur, fine bones,
Eleven tiny skulls with yellow teeth—
Death fitted to digestion.
                         If steel and stones
Are what we love, let's swallow them, then gulp
Benignly like the owl, and send them forth,
As buildings, shapes, desires, moans and groans,
But made of us. Leavings should not be waste.
Or else, how should we bless what we receive?

## The Silver Leaf

The silver that shies off the silver-leaf maple,
In the wind that planes through like an
    express,
At the expectation of rain, in change,
Is a change like that of a man, turned over,
Out of sodden sun and clouds, to feel,
On his other silver side, his strife,
His quick veins shying in the wind's war.

## December Storm

Deceitful snow, made of the gray sea,
Half water and half ice—the wind
Screams we must have it, and a rage
Of indecision blinds the world,
Colder than death; but it will end.
We will look up and see again;
Having been whipped across the eyes
Like penitents, to make us see.

## Town Meeting

The meeting's in order. What's coming? What's
    to come?
The health officer says death. The carpenter

Says everything is shipshape. The minister
Says God—we try to say it too, like that,
But a frog croaks in our throats. Then nobody
    speaks.
For weeks. Isn't there something we mean to
    say?
Is the coming never to be come to? Speak!
Mr. Moderator, don't hold him down—the
    spark,
The star, the old, love-flinted animal.
Don't stop him saying what we knew before
    we came.


## Sent Ahead

Praise, hard as that is in a world where fires
Are set by death and not eternity.
But what else? Before the man or dog expires,
The dog star sails, the man star rides its sea.
We have been sent ahead long since, wherever
Fire dives. Our sky is not a crossbar tree
For rags to rot on. Praise; burn; follow whatever
Springs. I praise the star that slings my body free.


## Life Must Burn

Blood locked as I am, sun bound, and hot
    as a pistol,
There is nothing for it but to burn.
The sweat a man wipes off his brow is so
    much water
Under the bridge. Nothing is stern
Or rock bound. There are no more umbrageous
    willows.
The dust is hot. Take it from there.
Deserts of anger lie ahead. The wind is riling.
Warm up to it. Never take care.

ROBERT SILLIMAN HILLYER was born in East Orange, N. J., in 1895. His publications include novels, translations, and poetry, the most recent volume of the latter being *The Suburb by the Sea*. Mr. Hillyer, a Pulitzer Prize winner, is a member of the National Institute of Arts and Letters, a fellow of the American Academy of Arts and Sciences, a chancellor of the Academy of American Poets, and President of the Poetry Society of America. He lives in Greenwich, Conn., and is at present a Visiting Professor at the University of Delaware.

## Intermezzo

By the lake the orchards lie
Half in shadow, half in sun.
We were mortal, you and I;
We were parted. Now, as one,
We leave the shadow for the sun.

When I died I walked away
Down a long suburban street
Where the feathery elms of May
Arched as in a forest aisle.
There I walked as evening fell
Knowing that we two would meet
When the sickle moon was curled
Round the windmill by the well.

And you whispered with a smile,
"If you waken, you will weep;
That was in another world;
Now lie down, lie down and sleep."

Princess, if the lakes were dry,
And the orchard paths were frozen,
Would you still, unchanged as I,
Choose the lover you have chosen?

# In the Shadowy Whatnot Corner

Blest be the bric-a-brac that still survives
Demolished houses and forgotten lives,
And, with a Dresden signal from the shelves,
Calls back the children who were once
    ourselves.
The French clock swings the mercury of time
Captive in glass and regular as rhyme.
The candelabra in their crystal lustres
Splinter a beam of light in rainbow clusters.
Swans die in their own music, roses in
Their own perfume, but roses from Pekin
And swans from Sèvres, having no scent or
    song,
Stay, while a hundred summers glide along.

Lovers from Meissen, clowns from
    Copenhagen,
Amorous cupids, innocently pagan,
Beribboned shepherds with their shepherdesses
Poised in forever unachieved caresses:
These beings, like ourselves, were shaped
    from clay,
But in such heat as burned their lusts away.
Frozen in flame, they glazed to chilly fire,
Immune from death and death's pale twin,
    desire,
Unless, on some dyspeptic morning, Sadie's
Wild duster tangles in the porcelain ladies,
Or Mrs. Fulsome, clumsy connoisseur,
As usual breaks what most appeals to her.

Tiffany glass, they tell me with a smile—
In fact, all *art nouveau*—is back in style.
The eighteen-forties, too, come in for praise,
Late Empire, and my opalescent vase,
Which makes me wonder where such things
    would be
If Style had swept the previous century.

The architect, to serve the vogue, uptilts
Greenhouses thirty stories high on stilts,
Supplanting walls of stone with sheets of glass.
Like "General Grant" and mansard these will
    pass,
While, cherished and unchanging, will remain
The only world that lasts—of porcelain.

JOHN HOLMES, born in Somerville, Mass., in 1904, has been editor, anthologist, and lecturer as well as teacher and poet. His books of poetry include *Address to the Living, Fair Warning, Map of My Country,* and *The Double Root,* and he has edited *The Poet's Work, The Complete College Reader,* and *A Little Treasury of Love Poems.* A member of Phi Beta Kappa, he is New England Vice-President of the Poetry Society of America, and lives in Medford, Mass., where he is an Associate Professor of English at Tufts College.

➤➤➤-➤➤➤-➤➤➤-➤➤➤-➤➤➤-➤➤➤-➤➤➤-➤➤➤-➤➤➤-➤➤◄◄◄-◄◄◄-◄◄◄-◄◄◄-◄◄◄-◄◄◄-◄◄◄-◄◄◄-◄◄◄-◄◄◄

## *Pour Down*

The wells of air pour down
Winds from the fourth quarter,
And at the first turning
Come cold for a farewell.
In the second season sunfall
Yellows the thin wash of air,
Then forecast summer comes true,
Fruit forms, the tipping leaf
Turns in the fine heat, and
The wells of air pour down
Winds from the fourth quarter.
Almanac, not rehearsal.
Stones surface, boughs rot,
As it was in the beginning.
Prepare. Prepare. Nothing
Else? Drink these and wells
That pour, divide, and speak
From root-ache, blood-need,
The years-without-end Eden.
And after? From the mind of men
Color, speed, dimension,
The wells of his offering,
Pour down.

85

# Bucyrus

A slant-windowed belt-footed enormously
  long-boomed
Digger, dignified or at least designated as Lima—
That's a place in Peru. What is Lima doing here,
Clawing at Alewife Brook, to lay its water away
In five-foot-round adequate concrete tunnels?
    The alewife, Indian for a sort of herring,
    Maybe meaning aloof, swarmed up
      this stream.
    They named it who netted a health here.
Bucyrus, a steam-shovel redder than two
  freight cars,
Hero of tar-paper bunkhouses in the log-boom
  country;
A big-bucketted up-biter, grunting soft-coal
  smoke,
He jumbled boulders and raw fill into dinkey-
  trains
That hauled it through 1910 to build build a dam.
    In the Deerfield East Branch, fish were pike,
    Perch, bass, mostly pike big and criminal,
    The bass flat the other way, a few lost trout.
Bucyrus worked three years to chew up enough
  Vermont
To dam a river. While he snored in the peeled-
  pine night
You there could stare at cold air. You could
  see the
Dead trees out in the water stood up for how
  hard it is
To kill fish, and get running water under
  control.
    Bucyrus the whale, grounded and dry-
      mouthed,
    Tried, and Lima, a Diesel female and nervous,
    Is trying, but the ancient stream runs, water
    Is not to be buried, and the boulders will drift.

# The Letter

Childe Harold to the dark tower, L–two
Four turns, R–three, and the notches
Lined up. I guess through beveled glass
Miracles by mail, air-mail, all mine,
Checks and love, if dial to dial matches.

Silent as a safe-cracker, I twirl and try,
Intent as the other burglars, and ah! it
Opens. They too break in on their lives.
They clutch stuffing from the mailbags.
Rip and read, then and there, no matter
   what.

They stand around like the spaced columns
That hold up public buildings, stunned
By something not in, or in, the envelope.
They go away, and more move up, robbers
Rubbing the dials for a break long planned.

I never read letters in the post office.
I carry them to the cottage. There, alone,
I divide the loot with myself, not fifty-fifty.
Counterfeit. Dead-end. Non-negotiable.
But one is currency. One is mine. One.


# The Overgrown Back Yard

There is a rumor hereabout of summer,
A long green and heavy heat,
By thunder sometimes broken asunder,
And rivers in the street.

But early in the season, with reason,
We began with weapons war
On weeds rising, on the lilac raising
New leaves too far.

Wet makes the grass grow. Sun, we
    think,
Drinks up the damp. Whet we
Then the hand-sickle against the fickle
Grass, and cut.

The sickle sound, close to the ground,
Is soft. The hooked blade's bevel
Makes fall the grass, that eye may pass
On lawn at level.

That insistent goer, the charging
    mower,
Hauls back, and pants, and lunges
At tufts and patches. The wheel catches.
But the green changes

From jungle creeping up, to dingle,
To a dell. This clothesyard slope,
From under cover, with this going over,
Begins to take shape.

JOSEPHINE (Mrs. Eric) JACOBSEN was born in Coburg, Canada, in 1908. She has published three books of poetry, *Let Each Man Remember, For the Unlost,* and *The Human Climate,* and her poems have appeared in *Hopkins Review, Poetry, Voices,* and numerous other periodicals. Mrs. Jacobsen won the Louise Imogen Clark Award, given by the Poetry Society of America, lists her occupation as Writer, and lives in the winter in Baltimore, and in the summer in Whitefield, N. H.

# For Any Member of the Security Police

### I

Let us ask you a few questions, without rancor,
In simple curiosity, putting aside
Our reactions or the rising of our gorge,
As a child asks, How does it work? As premise:

Some limitations you admit; soundproofing
Is never perfect, hints rise from any cellar;
There are a few—a very few—for whom
   reshaping
Must be abandoned for that catchall, death.

The capitulation-point, (call it $X_2$)
In very strong young men, well-fed and finicky,
Is sometimes unbelievably delayed.
Most are much easier: women they love,

The children from their body's seed, are
   garden-paths
To the objective. And humiliation
After the first betrayal, serves as breach
So that all others follow fairly freely.

We haven't yet discussed the top success,
The mind's invasion; that fierce citadel
Proverbially adamant to rack and fire,
To conjuration, sometimes even to love,

Now, by a postern-door, all solved so simply.
Nothing more formidable than a needle,
A pellet; the kindly country-doctor's tools.
Now, with this data in mind, if you could tell
   us . . .

## II

Is there routine in this, like unlocking the desk
And running through the Baskets, In and Out,
Uncovering the typewriter: Memo to Miss Prout:
*How was our average on yesterday's task?*

The season must sometime be April, fair beyond
   fiction,
The inner crocus, enamel; the apple-trees
Fierce with fragrance and strength. You must
   move among these
In the common lot. Are you dogged by a minor
   friction?

When in at your window starlight is spilt
From the midnight sky, and you, still watcher, see
The moon in silence pass each boundary,
The moon, who never will acknowledge guilt;

When your two hands, fresh from their late
   employ,
Touch in the dark your lover's body, after;
When in the first hot sun climbs her clear
   laughter,
Do you meet the simplicity of joy?

And when the ambiguous bird in the dark
   meadow
Cries out an undecipherable message
And utter stillness is the moment's presage
When there shall bend above you a chill shadow,

Then are you lonely only as all are lonely
Leaving the loved and known, or do you see
A small, unnatural eternity
Shaped otherwise, and fashioned for you only?

GALWAY KINNELL was born in 1927 in Pawtucket, R. I.
Poems by him have appeared in the *Beloit Poetry Journal* and
in *New World Writing*. He lives in Chicago, and is Director
of the Liberal Arts Programs of the Downtown Center of the
University of Chicago.

❧❧❧❧❧❧❧❧❧❧❧❧❧❧❧❧❧❧❧❧❧❧❧

## First Song

Then it was dusk in Illinois, the small boy
After an afternoon of carting dung
Hung on the rail fence, a sapped thing
Weary to crying. Dark was growing tall
And he began to hear the pond frogs all
Calling upon his ear with what seemed their joy.

Soon their sound was pleasant for a boy
Listening in the smoky dusk and the nightfall
Of Illinois, and then from the field two small
Boys came bearing cornstalk violins
And rubbed three cornstalk bows with resins,
And they set fiddling with them as with joy.

It was now fine music the frogs and the boys
Did in the towering Illinois twilight make
And into dark in spite of a right arm's ache
A boy's hunched body loved out of a stalk
The first song of his happiness, and the song
  woke
His heart to the darkness and into the sadness
  of joy.

## Island of Night

In a dream I saw a beautiful island
Surrounded by an abrasive river;
And soon it was all rubbed into river and
Gone forever, even the sweet millet and
  the clover.

The next dream was night. Out of dark caves
Poured the thunder of horses; and across
    the black
Desert at the touch of their shattering hooves
Hundreds of colors were blooming—beau-
    tiful, fantastic.

I awoke and touched you and your eyes
    opened
Into the river of darkness around us,
And we were together and love happened.
Now I do not wonder that men should bless

The down-tearing gods, who also let us lift
Islands of night against their downward
    drift.

## A Walk in the Country

We talked all morning, she said
The day's nice, on this nice summer
Day let's walk where birds glide
At berries ripening everywhere.
And I thought, is it only me such
Beauty refuses to touch?

But I walked all the same, to please
What only an arm held close,
Through a green wood to a space
Where grass was turned over by a
    farmer whose
Rickety horses ploughed
While the crow and robin sang out loud.

She said it was nice. It was.
But I could hear only in the close
Green around me and there in the dark
Brown ground where I stood, a meadowlark
Or other thing speak sharp of shortness
That takes us all and under like that
    grass.

# Passion

At the end of a full day of walking we found
A good hill for our camp, and we ate
By the low fire and sat up to wait
For the stars and the embers, but it was not late
When the sound of our love was the only sound.

Then we were quiet together, like a footfall,
A long time vibrant on the pine-needled
   ground,
Your warm person touching me, and in the
   air around
A flute of memory joining the sound
Of your breathing and the noise of some small
   animal . . .

Overhead the stars hung in their right course.
Hours later a mourning dove stirred the night
With soft speech. I was deaf, and the light
Marking the east fell on extinguished sight.
My new eyes searched the passion of the stars.


# To William Carlos Williams

*(After a lecture at a school of English)*

When you came and you talked and
   you read with your
Private zest from the varicose marble
Of the podium, the lovers of literature
Paid you the real tribute of their almost
   total
Inattention—although one woman when
   you spoke of a pig
Did squirm, and it is only fair to report
   another gig-

gled. But you didn't even care. You seemed
Above remarking we were not your friends.
You hung around inside the rimmed
Circles of your heavy glasses and smiled and
So passed a lonely evening. In an hour
Of talking your honesty built you a tower.

When it was over and you sat down and
    the chair-
man got up and smiled and congratulated
You and shook your hand, I watched a
    professor
In neat bow tie and enormous tweeds,
    who patted
A faint praise of the sufficiently damned,
Drained spittle from his pipe, then
    scrammed.


## For the Lost Generation

Oddities composed the sum of the news.
$E=mc^2$
Was another weird
Evidence of the existence of Jews.

And Paris! All afternoon in someone's attic
We raised our glasses
And drank to the asses
Who ran the world and turned neurotic.

Ours was a wonderful party.
Everyone threw rice,
The fattest girls were nice,
The world was rich in wisecracks and
    confetti.

The war was a first wife, somebody's
    blunder,
Who was right, who lost,

Held nobody's interest,
The dog on top was as bad as the dog
    under.

Sometimes after whisky, at the break
    of day,
There was a weary look, trace
Of a tear on a face,
Face of the blue nights that were wing-
    ing away.

Look back on it all, the faraway cost—
Crash and sweet blues
(O Hiroshima, O Jews)—
No generation was so gay as the lost.


## Spring Oak

Above the quiet valley and unrippled lake
While woodchucks burrowed new holes, and
    birds sang,
And radicles began downward and shoots
Committed themselves to the spring
And entered with tiny industrious earthquakes,
A dry-rooted, winter-twisted oak
Revealed itself slowly. And one morning
When the valley underneath was still sleeping
It shook itself and was all green.


## Chicago

### 1

In this city I loved you, where light
Struggles in the gulf of evening,
Shadow of the earth you left, who sang
A candle voice in its dark streets.

95

Those left behind pick of opposite dooms.
Neon flames, jazz trumpets the marihuana
   sex.
Dark beyond; a train scours El tracks
Hour after hour, mirroring gloom.

I imagine that whenever at night a plane
Settles over this hive Chicago,
Those looking down protest it is not so . . .
But the dark is old and its maggots thicken.

2

But, though jazz was burning when we
   obeyed,
In tears, the darkness, and neon lit veins
   of the city,
We found in twilight something, shadow
   of beauty,
Cast before sunrise by the candles of
   day.

So when I leave what I discovered here,
   and the plane
Climbs some dusk over a shrinking town,
This kindling darkness, I will look down
And see them in towers in the hush of evening,

The lights breaking up and down the cells
   of Chicago,
And watch them fade and mingle, every-
   thing we have done,
Bright wilderness, city of night, and up
   there alone
Revive the embrace in that melted glow.

AUDREY (Mrs. Curtiss) McGAFFIN was born in Baltimore, Md., in 1914. She has published poems in *Imagi, Voices, Talisman, Epos, Spirit,* and *Saturday Evening Post,* and won the Chandler Memorial Award, and the Midwest Writers' Conference Prize Award. Her present home is in Baltimore.

## At Cambridge

This is the hand
that planted a vine
that covered the iron
that enclosed the land
that cherished tradition
within the mansion
loved by the mind that pride filled.

This is the land
that nourished the vine
that rusted the iron
and rotted the mansion
that housed tradition
loved by the mind
that directed the pride that the
    hand killed.

## Inertia

Nothing wild—
and woolly fog
enfolds this game, clogged
with a lull and a yawn
and a lukewarm luck
that warms no bones.

The dirty
dog-eared back
of the day, like a card
cast from the deck,

**97**

lies on the lake,
and its two-spot eyes
stare at the sky
but take in no trick.

The doldrums
have dealt this deuce
of a dull day. . . .

## Avalon

Now, night; and once again
She moves among star-prisons isolate
As islands in a dark-blue water, turns her
    face
Toward land and lake. I stand beneath
The trees that hide her whiteness, brightness
From me, yet I see her islanded
And mirrored in this glassy frame, and
    know
The white hind leaps through appleboughs
There, unattainable, inviolate.

And I shall never walk
Her spiraled pathway, straight as horn
Of unicorn, while basely bodied thus
Imprisoned more than stars, blue-bound
By night, by mirror-moat, and
Surely bound by earth. She waits,
Threefold a goddess, shrine, and silver caer,
Forgot in present time by all but
Madmen, poets, and the dead,
And this, her priestess and her daughter.

JAMES MERRILL was born in New York City in 1926. He has published one book, *First Poems*, and has won the Blumenthal, Levenson, and Harriet Monroe prizes given by *Poetry*. At present he lives in New York City.

‑⫸⫸‑⫸⫸‑⫸⫸‑⫸⫸‑⫸⫸‑⫸⫸‑⫸⫸‑⫸⫸‑⫸⫸‑⫸⫸‑⫷⫷‑⫷⫷‑⫷⫷‑⫷⫷‑⫷⫷‑⫷⫷‑⫷⫷‑⫷⫷‑⫷⫷‑⫷⫷‑

## *Olive Grove*

The blue wave's slumber and the rocky brow
Almost submerged where while her father
  slept
Sleep of the blue wave from his forehead
  leapt
The goddess, dropped her gift, this silvery
  bough,

On him who among olives drowses now
Among these drowsing boughs their trunks
  express,
Pale paint from tubes so twisted, emptiness
Might sooner have put forth the slumbering
  green

Than these whose gnarled millennium bestows
(Upon his slumber tentatively marine
For whom endurance, lacking theirs, had been
Too bare an ikon of the mind's repose)

A dream, not of his dreaming that would wean
Roots from deep earth, rather of how each
  delves
To taste infusions by whose craft ourselves,
Once dreams in the mind of earth, like olive-
  trees,

Houses, the sleeper and his smile, the quais
And tall sail bent on the blue wave, have grown
Out of the scalding center that alone
Is wakeful for its melting images.

99

# Hotel de l'Univers et Portugal

The strange bed, whose recurrent dream we are,
Basin, and shutters guarding with their latch
The hour of arrivals, the reputed untouched Square.
Bleakly with ever fewer belongings we watch
And have never, it each time seems, so coldly before

Steeped the infant membrane of our clinging
In a strange city's clear grave acids;
Or thought how like a pledge the iron key-ring
Slid overboard, one weighty calm at Rhodes,
Down to the vats of its eventual rusting.

And letters moulting out of memory, lost
Seasons of the breast of a snowbird . . .
One morning on the pillow shall at last
Lie strands of age, and many a crease converge
Where the ambitious dreaming head has tossed

The world away and turned, and taken dwelling
Within the pillow's dense white dark, has heard
The lover's speech from cool walls peeling
To the white bed, whose dream they were.
Bare room, forever feeling and annulling,

Bare room, bleak problem set for space,
Fold us ever and over in less identity
Than six walls hold, the oval mirror face
Showing us vacantly how to become only
Bare room, mere air, no hour and no place,

Lodging of change, and bleak as all beginning.
We had begun perhaps to lack a starlit Square.
But now our very poverties are dissolving,
Are swallowed up, strong powders to ensure
Sleep, by a strange bed in the dark of dreaming.

MARY (Mrs. Gilbert) MILLS was born in Milwaukee, Wis., in 1920. These are her first published poems. A housewife, Mrs. Mills has been a summer student at the Writers' Conference in the Rocky Mountains under the auspices of the University of Colorado. Her home is in Phoenix, Ariz.

# Fable

The bough will bend, the leaf will sometime fall,
the seed will flower, the acorn make an oak;
fledglings will learn to imitate the call
they hear; the axe will spend a stroke
to round the circle; bough, leaf, seed, and flower
follow in season; time owns not an end
nor measures the minutes out; who marks the hour
deludes himself; *I know* means *I pretend*.

The dial to gauge the sun should fear a cloud,
a clock depends for life upon a spring;
what shall remind the rude, the rough, the proud,
if clocks run down, or dials no sun can sing?
Look on the leaf, the flower, the oak, the bough:
there read the fable, time is always now.

# Pedigree

Wisdom, out of Anguish by Denial
foaled in December, aged a winter year
through one short month of discipline in
    trial
till freedom, not the bit, was more to fear.
Wisdom has a hard mouth.

# The White Horse

The white horse walked dry-shod across the
   mirror
an awful apparition; arched astride
that barebone steed, a skeleton of pride
whiter than hate, gaunt, spare, ungodly silent,

armed to the grinning canines, porting a
   trident;
scapulas, ribs, fibulas, femurs, lank
bone on lank bone, rider and ridden rank
noiselessly seeking their ghastly ghostly forage;

nothing to feed on save my coward courage
avid for flesh, discovering lonely bone,
courting Medusa, conquering only stone,
spectered and haunted mad with soundless
   terror,

driven to smash the blank unsilvered mirror.


# The White Peacock

On broad plains of bright sound
the white peacock preens
fanned brilliant blue greens
gleaming in tiers
on sunbent grass.

Through wood, muted brass
to the last blatant phrase
the white peacock screams
in ardent self-praise.

But nobody sees, nobody hears.

# Garden Party

Dark is the house, the hall, the mirror silent
of image; out in the garden minor talent
loud with one picayune thought; the storm a
    sigh
cold in tall trees, the fading sunshine surly
folding the lonely, warming only the gallant;
old as the waning hour long shadows lie.

Bough on the bush for screen, there crouch
    the violent
mouthing their awe, doomed to dismissal early,
vowing faint fealty to idols bored and dry;
marking the proper time for departure, the
    valiant
retreat undefeated leaving the wet green curly
sod to the six o'clock vultures hovering nearby.


# The Library

Sun strikes those windows blind
that separate the stretched green world
    below,
mirrors of one mind
another asking, knowing that does not know

safe closed in red stone walls
while slant rain etches time on a dusty pane,
sounds unfeeling, falls
in an ideal world; in here it does not rain.

This is a brown-shelved ark
adrift on a dream in the blue opaque night
    air,
light in the wet warm dark
where the lions of Judah lie in their fusty lair.

103

# *Apostasy*

The day the wind is white shall I be free,
when green grass harshly old stiff underfoot
burns black overnight; cold water slows the root
growing down into it; aspens and birches pleat
all the steel sky through their own bare
    branches: be
but the skeleton, love, the flesh of summer loot
laid on the granite altars that have stood
centuries before and after us indeed.

Dying to freedom, then, being free and/or dead,
wanting my shackles back I kneel to pray
bent on the same stone where the trough ran
    red
under the brown bull's belly, the night and
    the day
seen one in the moon's eclipse, the sun inbred,
death and all winter absolutes at bay.


# *Postscript*

Now I have touched you near the grated bone
with a simple tale an idiot could write or read
told in the quiet repressive monotone
of fact beyond wildest fancy; out of my need
to make you feel the cold immortal stone,
the rock of reason lying half-hid in weed,
in every song I sing the undertone
from aeries where forbidden ravens breed.
Why should I grieve? Set music to the moan;
joy is not joy without sorrow; gall for mead,
the measure of heaven is hell; the very sea
moves over mountains man has never known.

MARIANNE MOORE was born in St. Louis, Mo., in 1887. Her books include *Observations, What are Years, Nevertheless,* and *Collected Poems.* Miss Moore won the Dial Award in 1924, and has subsequently added to her laurels the Harriet Monroe Award, the Bollingen Prize, the National Book Award, and the Pulitzer Prize, not to mention Honorary Doctorates in Literature from Wilson College, Mount Holyoke College, Dickinson College, and the University of Rochester. She lives in Brooklyn, and is at present engaged in translating the Fables of La Fontaine for The Viking Press.

## *Apparition of Splendor*

Partaking of the miraculous
    since never known literally,
Dürer's rhinoceros
    might have startled us equally
    if black-and-white-spined elaborately.

Like another porcupine, or fern,
    the mouth in an arching egret,
was too black to discern
    till exposed as a silhouette;
    but the double-embattled thistle of jet—

disadvantageous supposedly—
    has never shot a quill. Was it
some joyous fantasy
    plain eider-eared exhibit
    of spines rooted in the sooty moss,

or "train supported by porcupines—
    a fairy's eleven yards long"? . . .
as when the lightning shines
    on thistlefine spears, among
    prongs in lanes above lanes of a shorter
      prong—

"with the forest for nurse"—also dark
    at the base—where needle-debris
springs to hide each footmark;
    the setting for a symmetry
    you must not touch unless you are a fairy.

Maine should be pleased that its animal
    is not a waverer, but rather
than fight, lets the primed quill fall.
    Shallow oppressor, intruder,
    insister, you have here a resister.


## *Then the Ermine:*

"rather dead than spotted"; and
    believe it
        despite reason to think not,
I saw a bat by daylight;
hard to credit

but I know that I am right. It
    charmed me—
        wavering like a jack o' the green,
weaving about above me
insecurely.

Instead of hammer-handed bravado
    adopting force for fashion,
momentum with a motto:
*mutare sperno vel timere*

—I don't change, am hard to frighten
    if the meaning is not really
am I *craven?*
Nothing's certain.

Fail, and Lavater's physiography
    has another admirer
Of skill that axiomatically
flowers obscurely.

Both paler and purpler than azure,
    note marine
      uncompliance—bewarer
Of the weak analogy, between
waves in motion.

Change? Of course, if the palisandre
    settee can express
      for us, "ebony violet"—
Master Corbo in full dress
and shepherdess

at once—exhilarating hoarse crownote
    and dignity with intimacy.
Our foiled explosiveness is yet
a kind of prophet,

a perfecter, and so a concealer—
    with the power of implosion—
like violets by Dürer;
even darker.

HOWARD MOSS was born in New York City in 1922. He has published one book of poems, *The Wound and the Weather*, has won the Janet Sewell Davis Award from *Poetry*, and was Poetry Editor of the first issue of *New World Writing*. Poetry editor of *The New Yorker*, he lives in New York City.

## The Lie

Some bloodied sea-bird's hovering
  decay
Assails us where we lie, and lie
To make that symbol go away,
To mock the true north of the eye.
But lie to me, lie next to me;
The world is an infirmity.

Too much of sun's been said, too
  much
Of sea, and of the lover's touch,
Whole volumes that old men debauch.
But we, at the sea's edge curled,
Hurl back their bloody world.
Lie to me, lie next to me,

For there is nothing here to see
But the mirror of ourselves, the day,
Clear with the odors of the sea.
Lie to me. And lie to me.

## The Hermit

Always there is someone who has turned
  away
From the important mornings and the eve-
  ning's eye,
Who sits on the top of a tall stairway

Somewhere in the country, or at the edge
  of slums,
And lives there quietly, day after day,
And does not turn his head to look our way.

What made him leave our ashes and our love?
Did the open sky above the city tempt
His mortal senses to the green, unkempt
Free countryside? And now to disappoint him
The leaves are shy, and the birds
Go about their nests and songs.

Loving the mountains, hating the shore,
Wherever he is, he is not far
From whatever it is that brought him there.
Left in a circle of deserted air,
He draws the edges round him like a tent
  to hide
The wanderer, traveling inside.

His eyes are wild, his island is insane,
We say, and envy secretly his deeper calm.
He calls it home. Perhaps inverted pride,
Pursued in childhood, was his suicide;
Or maybe once, walking in a crowd,
He shuddered at the passion at his side.

Dressed for a battle that has taken place,
Or will never happen, he masks his face
Against the hostile, preferring the alone.
Tuning his armor to the distant guns,
He writes, in a circle, on his shield,
*O miseries and appetites of the world.*

PHILIP MURRAY was born in Philadelphia, Pa., in 1924. His poems have appeared in many magazines, including *Harper's, The New Yorker, Sewanee Review, Georgia Review, Imagi, Furioso, Voices*. He lives in Philadelphia, gives his chief occupation as Poet, and chief occupational hazard, Prose.

>>>->>>->>>->>>->>>->>>->>>->>>->>>->>>((-((-((-((-((-((-((-((-((-((-((-((-

## *In the Annals of Tacitus*

These Stoic Romans had a flair for dying;
Theirs was no hasty or shameful exit into darkness.
They contrived it often with an elaborate will,
Willfulness even, recognizing the freedom of death
From which no tyrannies deprived them.

And since it was their ultimate achievement
They considered carefully how best to accomplish
This last departure with skilled and valorous
    mien,
Whether to the land of gods, the seas of nothing
Or to the nameless wonder behind the skies.

With equal mind and resolute gestures,
Studied but none the less sincere for that,
They fell upon their swords or opened their veins,
Discarding life as a swimmer discards his clothes
To meet the water naked when he dives.

They bore death as a woman bears a child
With such strict agony of purpose and repose
That history pauses still upon their noble names.

## *Carrara*

Art has taught this man to writhe in marble
With his agony flowing behind him,
A fountain where frozen water plays
His disconsolate music. Locked in stone,
His body is naked to all weather;
His sorrow, motionless in calm or storm,

A petrified rhythm of desire
That once, forever, determined his pose.
Still he is cold to touch and his secret is
Not to be forced or kissed to life;
The Furies despise him ineffectually
And Death envies his unyielding poise—
Carrara, instructed, immaculate,
Is permanent; study this marble man.

## The Turning

It was a day of turning when you came—
The clouds were rolling in the shifting sky;
The sun was spinning on the garden lawn
A net of leaf-light cast for your dark hair.
It was a day of movement everywhere—
The hills were dipping, rising, the river ran,
Leaped, molded to rocks, and leaped again.
I felt the very earth beneath my feet then
Wheeling away to other parts of the world
In that one moment I would have caught
and held.

## The Finches

*(Zoological Gardens, Dominican Republic)*

They lined the long perches like a living color spectrum;
And they were always shifting, bright, light, fantastically
grained marbles,
Bobbing with stout, sharp, conical beaks shaped for
cracking the seeds of weeds,
Preening, smoothing, and dressing their soft, endlessly
shaded, variegated feathers.

There was the greenfinch decked in green and gold,
The goldfinch with his gold and black,
The purple finch, the chaffinch, and the musical marvel
bullfinch,
The male summer linnet in his crimson breast and crown,
The black-headed, rose-breasted hawfinch and
Even the Indian Amadavat, strawberry finch

**111**

Whose plumage is red and black flecked with white,
  whose vicious beak is red.

They danced and dazzled before me, rainbow of birds,
And I studied them long in the hot Dominican sun;
Oh I burned my eyes and I filled up my head like a cage.

## *A Little Litany to St. Francis*

St. Francis of the mountain cave and wattle hut,
          of the willow roofs and rush mats,
          of the rock and fountain,
          of the wheat field and the burning mountain,
          of the crossways and the lonely island,
          of the earthworm and the hungry robins,
          of the tame falcon that woke you for Matins,
          of the swallows of Alviano,
          of the sparrows of Bevagna,
          of the vineyards of Rieti,
            Teach us humility.

St. Francis of the pheasant and turtle dove,
          of the cicada in the olive grove,
          of the wild rabbit at Creccio,
          of the fierce wolf at Gubbio,
          of the fireflies by the river,
          of the fishes in the lake,
          of poplar and pine,
          of cypress and oak,
          of bush and berry,
          of the honey bee,
            Teach us simplicity.

St. Francis, poet and folk singer,
          of our brother Sun, our sister Moon,
          of our sister Water, our brother Fire,
          of our brother Wind and all weather,
          of our sister Earth, her fruits and flowers,
          of our sister Death, and the larks at
            Portiuncula singing when you died,
              Pray for us,
                  **AMEN**

112

LOUISE TOWNSEND NICHOLL was born in Scotch Plains, N. J. One of the founders of *The Measure,* one of the more distinguished little poetry magazines of the Twenties, she has published several volumes of poetry, *Water and Light, Dawn in Snow, Life is the Flesh,* and *The Explicit Flower.* She is an Associate Editor in the firm of E. P. Dutton & Co., who will publish her *Collected Poems* this fall.

->>>->>>->>>->>>->>>->>>->>>->>>->>>->>>-<<<-<<<-<<<-<<<-<<<-<<<-<<<-<<<-<<<-<<<-<<<-

## Color Alone Can Speak

Old looking glass grows darker, it is true,
But silicate nor silver can explain
What has engendered this unearthly hue
In antique mirror, where the windowpane
And world outside are shown so oddly blue.

A color integral eternally
Which down the centuries must trust its
        passage
To aging glass, elusive mercury,
The element elect for unknown message,
Arcanal, tinted with antiquity.

What color means, color alone can speak,
This is a blue which never has been spoken
And only by a brush's sentient stroke,
Half-hypnotized, intuitive, unbroken,
Could it be rescued, should the mirror break.

Poet amazed sees morning twice removed
Through glass and glass, but only paint can
        stay
This deep existence visioned and relived,
Or stanch the flowing of that blue away
Into a legend nevermore believed.

# Celestial Body

*"There are celestial bodies, and bodies terrestrial
. . . the glory of the celestial is one,
. . . the glory of the terrestrial . . . another."*

                                    I CORINTHIANS XV

The lens of morning, polished sheer by
   sleep
Shows the immortal essence housed in shape:
No longer wood but carpentered in mist
The unchanged contour of the bow-front
   chest,
Finished and turned exactly, to persist,
Facsimile forever to exist.

The lens of morning moving from the night
Resumes a closer and more usual sight:
Concept undying and celestial,
The mist, the substance of identity,
Gives place again to the terrestrial,
The pattern swirling in mahogany,
Irradiation from its temporal growing
And, like the other glory, past the knowing.

# Rondel for Middle Age

We play now very lightly, on the strings,
Meticulous, with infinite finesse.
Love was a symphony, the wind and brass
Throwing the thunder wide with stripéd
   wings,
But storm has softened into murmurings,
The careful modulations of caress:
We play now very lightly, on the strings,
Meticulous, with infinite finesse.

The bright bouquet of sound has lingerings
Of pastel tint and wildflower tenderness,
Hepatica, anemone, or less.
Love is returning to its earliest springs,
We play now very lightly, on the strings.

# Cigar Smoke, Sunday, After Dinner

Smell of cigar smoke, Sunday, after dinner,
Our eyes upon the visitor, leaning back
From robust lengthy elegance of dining,
White fingers catching up the golden slack
Of watch chain slung across expansive chest,
Rippling the links into a silken banner . . . .
All else was solid, black and white and shining,
The polished shirt-front and the black mustache,
Even the smooth fine broadcloth of the vest
Shone with a dark and unaccustomed luster.

Save that the damask throws a burnished flash,
The room, the coffee and the talk, are lost;
Only lives on the one compelling cluster,
The composition masterfully glossed,
Portrait of manhood and its ease of manner,
And how the white hand flicked away the ash.

# Cleavage

The storm had strong intention in its flow
And life was cleft forever in that winter,
A bound book falling open at its center
From the white thread of steady treadled snow.

Only a crystal stitching could divide
The pagination of such fibrous paper,—
The living web pressed out on time's long filter,—
And lay the two wings of the volume wide.

Schism from the sky, its high source hidden,
Provides no ground on which we can engage
The frigid arbiter, and we are liege
To turn the frozen pages, blindly bidden.

# Wild Cherry

## A Minor Threnody

The lot would be no loss, the slender stand
Of wild black cherry springing of themselves
In twos and threes, in sevens, and in twelves,
Stigmata of uncultivated land.

The lot's no good—better to have the money:
Fruit suited merely to a bird's quick need,
Even the blossom very small indeed
From which a bee takes only token honey.

Brittle but obdurate the grove had stood
Against the wind, or sprung again in haste
To mend its numbers, equalize the waste,
Working the simple sum as best it could.

But there's an algebra no tree can battle
Where the unknown is wealth instead of
  weather.
Remember well: the bloom was only feather,
And do not weep a woodland-in-the-little.

# Ornamental Water

The sheet of water which reflects the house
Laves in eternity its lovely theme;
The stone, worn fluid by long liquid use,
Bears the immortal dating of a dream.

Image unending, it will drowse and wake,
The undissolved reality enshrined
In that soft-shaken and remembering lake,
The ornamental water of the mind.

MARY ELIZABETH OSBORN was born at Margaretville in the Catskill Mountains of New York State. She is Professor of English at Hood College, Frederick, Md.

->>>->>>->>>->>>->>>->>>->>>->>>->>>->>>->><<<-<<<-<<<-<<<-<<<-<<<-<<<-<<<-<<<-<<<-<<<-

## Alma Mater

Welcome, boy, to these green fields,
take pasture here;
let delicate sheep-bells dull the blasts
and guilt of war.

Seek out the scholars' woodland which
philosophers desire;
here is a chart will lead you to
the shining tower

from whose deep windows locked in iron
comes the dead stare
of those who left humanity
and barred the door.

## Mid-Century

This whirlwind sounds a larger dissonance
Than has been heard in any fugue before;
Down broken streets patrol-car siren hunts
Through rubble fanged with fire.

Come back to the doomed house, elude the
    guard:
In this bright parlor you are safe from harm
Behind drawn curtains; play a harpsichord
And circumvent the storm.

# Thought for the Winter Season

In time of sorrow one should be
In a cold country, under sky
That has no passion; stripped boughs
Will not trouble the grieved eyes.

Snow on the meadows will retard
Torment of spring, no tropic word
Invade the mute, mountainous north;
The only speech be blizzard's breath.

Who touches the numbed field will find
Hypnotic ice that locks the ground,
And, fending frost in his own lungs,
Be reconciled to living things.

# Rural Legend

Systolic city noise denies the thrush,
But the antique, unseen flute, aerial-fresh,
Circles the lonely valley, the wasted farms,
Stirring forgotten pastures and weed-grown
    streams.

As an old man hobbles over his stony land,
Hearing the note, he whistles to echo the sound:
Wraiths of cattle graze, and the barns are filled;
Human children laugh from the sunken field.

Twilight thickens; something bulks in the mist:
Loping, savage strides of a half-tamed beast
Quicken, he scents mankind; and the pounding
    hoof
Seeks each crevice and rock: there is nowhere safe.

What is it moves through the shaggy mountain
    slope
And the darkened, whispering hollows robbed
    of sleep?
Is there anyone left alive who knows or cares
That the bird has roused the god-with-pointed-
    ears?

H. A. PINKERTON (Mrs. Wesley Trimpi) was born in Butte, Mont., in 1927. Her poems have appeared in *Twelve Poets of the Pacific, New Mexico Quarterly Review,* and *Pacific Spectator*. She has won both the Yvor Winters Poetry Prize and a Stanford University Creative Writing Fellowship. At present she is a graduate student at Radcliffe, Cambridge, Mass.

-》》-》》-》》-》》-》》-》》-》》-》》-》》-》》-《《-《《-《《-《《-《《-《《-《《-《《-《《-《《-

## *Degrees of Shade*

*Sic autem se habet omnis creatura ad Deum, sicut aer ad solem illuminantem.*

s.t., I, 104, *i*.

Our darkness stays, the only dark we know,
And I ever desiring to be right
Am ever more removed, conceiving not—
As foot can feel the earth and hand, the
   snow,
And still be unaware—I iive in light,
Within yet wilfully without Your thought.

Your partial absence, as a shade, extends
Upon the brightness that my will obscures.
I am confounded by degrees of shade
And sometimes think the shade's arc
   reascends
To perfect separation. But I am Yours,
Though nothing, if again I am unmade.

I cannot do as some in rage have done,
Who hating love's compulsion love their
   hate
So much they slay themselves perfecting it.
The course must be endured that was
   begun
In shade's dominion and empowered so late
To move from out the darkness You
   permit.

119

# The Prism

Change is the circumstance of our delight—
The season's delicate advance, release
From deep desire, and its renewal, sweet
For having known the winter. Yet caprice,
A prism in the unchanging diamond's white,
Fires in identity's unburning peace.

Identity, known or unknown, survives
The lost, untempered anguish and the waste.
Its hardness holds, affirming him who grieves;
What he is not and is it says till death.
Then as a diamond when the cutter's chisel
    cleaves
It is a perfect whole or only dust.

Yet while we live we still are free to choose
In Christ's perfected death and resurrection
To see all minor deaths and thereby lose
Delight in change for final absolution;
Or we may wait the death none can refuse
Which will, itself, be in time's disposition.

But righteousness, the days that we have spent
Learning the oldest speech, the simplest act,
Has only sanctity of precedent
Unless against time's claim of absolute
Spirit should be His flesh—not habitant—
And rest, itself unchanged, in time's estate.

## Error Pursued

Guilt unavowed is guilt in its extreme.
It still accumulates with strict regard
For time and act, although you cannot
    name
The creditor you owe. And your supreme
Defiance stirs rough gestures that have
    marred
Your art beyond repair or graceful shame.

Arrogance is a pose disclosing fear
Of law, whose constancy will let you die.
Nor mind nor body is your own to bend
In final alteration; even here,
Where the offending will would still deny
Dependence, know denial too must
    end.


## Deprivation

Continual deprivation, now,
Where hope was possibility
When innocence could still endow
The growing heart with charity.

The unbent head wins at the cost
Of that which it would overthrow.
Anguish affirms what has been lost,
What innocence could never know.

Can pride allay the separation,
Comfort the one who will endure,
Who gives no other affirmation
Than love's retractless forfeiture?

KENNETH PORTER was born in 1905 in Sterling, Kans. In addition to books of biography and history, he has published two books of verse, *The High Plains,* and *No Rain from These Clouds.* Mr. Porter now lives in Eugene, Ore., where he is a Senior Associate of the Business History Foundation.

>>>->>>->>>->>>->>>->>>->>>->>>->>>->>>->>>>((-<<<-<<<-<<<-<<<-<<<-<<<-<<<-<<<-<<<-<<<-<<<

## Thistle, Yarrow, Clover

I cross a weedy meadow
casting my sunset shadow

on thistle, yarrow, clover:
I name them over and over.

I hear a bobwhite's whistle
in clover, yarrow, thistle,

and pass a rusty harrow
in thistle, clover, yarrow.

My twilight vision follows
the twisting flight of swallows,

the nighthawk's swoop and hover
above the fields whose cover

is all a fading bristle
of yarrow, clover, thistle.

My dimming sight shall narrow
on clover, thistle, yarrow:

thistle, yarrow, clover—
I name them over and over.

# Beaver Sign

### (South Platte, Colorado)

Tramping the right-of-way
of the torn-up narrow-gauge
to the ghost-town Strontia Springs—
soon drowned by a reservoir—
we paused by an alder, gnawed
through near the root, and stripped
of twigs and leaves, the trunk
half-severed. The wide white water
showed no site for a beaver-dam.
Perhaps a wandering bachelor,
housed in a hole in the bank,
had stopped for a hasty lunch—
or just for exercise.

To me, however, it seemed
a calling-card from the past,
a narrow doorway on
more spacious days long-gone.
Did Carson, Bridger, Baker,
or Beckwourth, mulatto squawman
and Crow chief, sink their sticks
in these waters? I know my ear
bent to the stump could hear
the trappers' campfire talk,
and that by gazing through
the arch of the stub and stalk
I saw the *rendezvous*.

DACHINE RAINER was born in New York City in 1921. She
has edited, with Holley Cantine, *Prison Etiquette*, an anthology
of writings by American conscientious objectors, and has pub-
lished in *Retort, Golden Goose, Epoch, Imagi,* and other maga-
zines. She is an editor of *Retort Magazine*, and lives in Bears-
ville, N. Y.

>>>->>>->>>->>>->>>->>>->>>->>>->>>->>>K<<<-<<<-<<<-<<<-<<<-<<<-<<<-<<<-<<<-<<<-<<<

## *Samis Idyll*

I love as though I were not born to die
To be bettered by perversity, or feel pain.
Sharp is the dune grass, the blue Bay endless.
Long is my love, high my desire.

Wide-winged, the gull, when its desire is high
Flies the endless changing Bay, no rain
Pours on this flight, motion has no recourse.
I love as though I had not drowned, nor
    known fire.

Long is my love, high my desire.
The brackish pale-green cactus bites
    wonders,
The fish skulls bleach white on the white
    grains.
I love as though I were not born to die.

Gentle, impersonal, the waters in Gardiner's
    Bay
Enter, the boundaries disappear; landless,
    on the wane,
We move naked, incorporeal. Send us
Hot, cool, loved, free, with our desire high.

For however we dissemble, the feigned world
    is prior—
Its people and things—to this, where every sense
Proclaims the absence of change and pain.
Here we can love until we have to die.

# Ashokan

*"The lake is now 28 miles long, and at the edge, on these stones where we sit, is the site of one of the farmhouses of the village . . . they are all under the lake."*

**S. G. AT ASHOKAN RESERVOIR, N. Y.**

The village is submerged, houses and creatures
Lead a damp, indistinguishable life,
Communicating by subtle devices, their ingenuous
Dark demands of each other.

O a snake, a snake: there! quick! swimming
In two worlds—head in air, perplexed at voices,
His body fondled by the patroness of serpents,
In the damp, in the dark world of a cave.

O this village had lovers, had gardens, had dogs:
I hear an ancient child in the trespass
Of the irrational loon! Lilacs and trees
Edge the damp, dark world of a cave.

I hear their preoccupations: the underworld politics
Of love and its deaths, a *communitas* of serpents
    and men.
Children weave warily among the weeds
In the damp, dark world of a cave.

Their voices, dank and shrill with despair at
    Becoming,
Or rare and dim at Ending, settle at dusk.
And we sit above, communicating by subtle devices
Our ingenuous dark demands of each other.

# At Eighty-seven

Feelings are perceived as vague as limbs in my
    dismembered past
a haze of beings through which the I lived, and
    somehow lived them out;
now I hold, *sub specie aeternitatis,* the last place
    for the last life.

My name and circumstance—that is, daughter of,
    wife, mother of—
is cut into this standing reddish stone; there is
no object here unknown to those who live within
    this place:

clusters of stones and a few markers
for the two-hundred-year elders
separating rocks and grass between the nebulae.

From my as yet uninhabited place, Burial Hill
looks down on Red's Pond, and the other way
it monuments the wharves, the sails, the bay.

It is a good place: blue and green in spring,
lilacs and funereal wistaria, and always this
    reddish stone.
it waits. Meanwhile I seem surrounded by
    regenerations

of my atrophying,—beings emerge from one life
    after another,—
my daughters and theirs, theirs and their husbands
and other mothers and many solicitudes.

They speak haltingly, unnatural and perplexed,
I must live through their heads too knowingly,—
at eighty-seven they will remember mine.

But through this mist, of which weather is the
    fog always,
they seem to only talk of weather sharply as
    through some clear
ancient days: are you chill? Mother, do you wish
    another comforter?

Another comforter? Man sews at these.
Not from patches and scraps of cloth can filter
    such green
and lilac through this weathered brain—there are
    no yew trees.

The elders find them chill, I think.

THEODORE ROETHKE was born in Saginaw, Mich., in 1908. His books of poems are *Open House, The Lost Son and Other Poems, Praise to the End!* and the latest, *The Waking; Poems 1933-1953*, published by Doubleday. He has won the Eunice Tietjens and Levenson prizes awarded by *Poetry*, an award of the American Academy of Arts and Letters, and a Guggenheim Fellowship. He is Professor of English at the University of Washington.

## Song for the Squeeze-box

It wasn't Ernest; it wasn't Scott,
The boys I knew when I went to pot—
They didn't boast; they didn't snivel,
But stepped right up and swung at the Devil;
And after exchanging a punch or two,
They all sat down like me and you
—And began to drink up the money.

It wasn't the Colony; it wasn't the Stork;
It wasn't the joints in New York, New York;
But me and a girl friend learned a lot
In Ecorse, Toledo, and Wyandotte
—About getting rid of our money.

It was jump-in-the-hedge; it was wait-in-
the-hall;
It was "Would you believe it—*fawther's* tall!"
(It turned out she hadn't a father at all)
—But how she could burn up the money!

A place I surely did like to go
Was the underbelly of Cicero;
And East St. Louis and Monongahela
Had the red-hot spots where you feel a
—Lot like losing some money.

Oh, the Synco Septet played for us then,
And even the boys turned out to be men

**127**

As we sat there drinking that bathtub gin
—And loosened up with our money.

It was Samoots Matuna and Bugs Moran;
It was Fade me another and Stick out your
can;
It was Place and Show and Also Ran
—For you never won with that money.

Oh, it wasn't a crime, it wasn't a sin,
And nobody slipped me a Mickey Finn,
For whenever I could, I dealt them all in
—On that chunk of Grandpa's money.

It was Dead Man's Corner, it was Kelly's
Stable;
It was Stand on your feet as long as you're
able,
But many a man rolled under the table
—When he tried to drink up the money.

To some it may seem a sad thing to relate,
The dough I spent on Chippewa Kate,
For she finally left town on the Bay City
freight
—When she thought I'd run out of money.

The doctors, the lawyers, the cops are all
paid—
So I've got to get me a rich ugly old maid
Who isn't unwilling, who isn't afraid
—To help me eat up her money.

## Frau Bauman, Frau Schmidt, and Frau Schwartze
### (Scene: A Greenhouse in My Childhood)

Gone the three ancient ladies
Who creaked on the greenhouse ladders,
Reaching up white strings
To wind, to wind

The sweet-pea tendrils, the smilax,
Nasturtiums, the climbing
Roses, to straighten
Carnations, red
Chrysanthemums; the stiff
Stems, jointed like corn,
They tied and tucked—
These nurses of nobody else.
Quicker than birds, they dipped
Up and sifted the dirt;
They sprinkled and shook;
They stood astride pipes,
Their skirts billowing out wide into tents,
Their hands twinkling with wet;
Like witches they flew along rows,
Keeping creation at ease;
With a tendril for needle
They sewed up the air with a stem;
They teased out the seed that the cold
    kept asleep—
All the coils, loops, and whorls.
They trellised the sun; they plotted for
    more than themselves.

I remember how they picked me up, a
    spindly kid,
Pinching and poking my thin ribs
Till I lay in their laps, laughing,
Weak as a whiffet;
Now, when I'm alone and cold in my bed,
They still hover over me,
These ancient leathery crones,
With their bandannas stiffened with sweat,
And their thorn-bitten wrists,
And their snuff-laden breath blowing
    lightly over me in my first sleep.

# The Dance

Is that dance slowing in the mind of man
That made him think the universe could hum?
The great wheel turns its axle when it can:
I need a place to sing, and dancing-room,
And I have made a promise to my ears
I'll sing and whistle romping with the bears.

For they are all my friends: I saw one slide
Down a steep hillside on a cake of ice.—
Or was that in a book? I think with pride:
A caged bear rarely does the same thing twice
In the same way: O watch his body sway!—
This animal remembering to be gay.

I tried to fling my shadow at the moon,
The while my blood leaped with a wordless song.
Though dancing needs a master, I had none
To teach my toes to listen to my tongue.
But what I learned there, dancing all alone,
Was not the joyless motion of a stone.

I take this cadence from a man named Yeats;
I take it, and I give it back again:
For other tunes and other wanton beats
Have tossed my heart and fiddled through
    my brain.
Yes, I was dancing-mad, and how
That came to be the bears and Yeats would know.


# The Partner

Between such animal and human heat
I find myself perplexed. What is desire?—
The impulse to make someone else complete?
That woman would set sodden straw on fire.
Was I the servant of a sovereign wish,
Or ladle rattling in an empty dish?

We played a measure with commingled feet:
The lively dead had taught us to be fond.
Who can embrace the body of his fate?
Light altered light along the living ground.
She kissed me close, and then did something else.
My marrow beat as wildly as my pulse.

I'd say it to my horse: we live beyond
Our outer skin. Who's whistling up my sleeve?
I see a heron prancing in his pond;
I know a dance the elephants believe.
The living all assemble! What's the cue?—
Do what the clumsy partner wants to do!

Things loll and loiter. Who condones the lost?
This joy outleaps the dog. Who cares? Who cares?
I gave her kisses back, and woke a ghost.
O what lewd music crept into our ears!
The body and the soul know how to play
In that dark world where gods have lost their way.

## The Sloth

In moving-slow he has no Peer.
You ask him something in his ear;
He thinks about it for a Year;

And then, before he says a Word
There, upside down (unlike a Bird)
He will assume that you have Heard—

A most Ex-as-per-at-ing Lug.
But should you call his manner Smug,
He'll sigh and give his Branch a Hug;

Then off again to Sleep he goes,
Still swaying gently by his Toes,
And you must know he knows he knows.

EDWIN ROLFE was born in Philadelphia, Pa., in 1909. His books of poems include *To My Contemporaries,* and *First Love;* he has also written mystery novels and short stories. He now lives in Los Angeles and is at work on a novel.

‹‹‹‹‹‹‹‹‹‹‹‹‹‹‹‹‹‹‹‹‹‹‹‹‹‹‹‹‹‹‹‹‹‹‹‹‹‹‹‹‹‹‹

# *A Poem to Delight My Friends Who Laugh at Science-Fiction*

That was the year
the small birds in their frail and delicate battalions
committed suicide against the Empire State,
having, in some never-explained manner,
lost their aerial radar, or ignored it.

That was the year
men and women everywhere stopped dying natural
    deaths.
The aged, facing sleep, took poison;
the infant, facing life, died with the mother in childbirth;
and the whole wild remainder of the population,
despairing but deliberate, crashed in auto accidents
on roads as clear and uncluttered as ponds.

That was the year every ship on every ocean,
every lake, harbor, river, vanished without trace;
and even ships docked at quays
turned over like wounded animals, harpooned whales, or
    Normandies.

Yes, and the civilian transcontinental planes
found, like the war-planes, the sky-lanes crowded
and, praising Icarus, plunged to earth in flames.

Many, mild stay-at-homes, slipped in bathtubs,
others, congenital indoors-men, descending stairs,
and some, irrepressible roisterers, playing musical chairs.
Tots fell from scooter cars and tricycles
and casual passersby were stabbed by falling icicles.

Ah, what carnage! It was reported
that even bicarb and aspirin turned fatal,
and seconal too, to those with mild headaches,
whose stomachs were slightly acid, or who found they
    could not sleep.
All lovers died in bed, as all seafarers on the deep.

Till finally the only people left alive
were the soldiers sullenly spread on battlefields
among the shell-pocked hills and the charred trees.
Thus, even the indispensable wars died of ennui.

But not the expendable conscripts: they remained as
    always.
However, since no transport was available anywhere,
and home, in any case, was dead, and bare,
the soldiers wandered eternally
in their dazed, early-Chirico landscapes,
like drunken stars in their shrinking orbits
round and round and round and round

and (since I too died in the world-wide suicide)
they may still, for all I know, be there.
Like forsaken chessmen abandoned by paralyzed players,
they may still be there,
may still be there.

MAY SARTON was born in Belgium in 1912. She has written several novels, the latest being *A Shower of Summer Days*, and has published three books of poetry, *Encounter in April*, *Inner Landscape*, and *The Lion and the Rose*. A new one, *The Land of Silence*, will appear soon. A winner of the Golden Rose Award of the New England Poetry Society, Miss Sarton is Briggs-Copeland Instructor of English at Harvard and Radcliffe. She was recently awarded Bryn Bawr College's Lucy Martin Donnelly Fellowship. Her residence is in Cambridge, Mass.

## Summer Music

Summer is all a green air—
From the brilliant lawn, sopranos
Through murmuring hedges
Accompanied by high poplars;
In fields of wheat, surprises;
Through faraway pastures, flows
In slow decrescendos.

Summer is all a green sound—
Rippling in the foreground
To that soft applause,
The foam of Queen Anne's lace.
Green, green in the ear
Is all we care to hear.
Until a field suddenly flashes
The singing with so sharp
A yellow that it smashes
Loud cymbals in the ear.
Minor has turned to major
As summer, lulling and so mild,
Goes golden-buttercup-wild.

# Prothalamium

How pure the hearts of lovers as they walk
Through the rich quiet fields
Where the stiff wheat grows heavy on the stalk
And over barley and its paler golds,
The air is bright—

Would touch it all, embrace, learn it by hand,
Plunging their faces into the thick grain,
To stroke as well as see the cow's soft flank,
To feel the beech trunk harsh under the palm,
And oh, to drink the light!

They do not even walk yet hand in hand,
But every sense is pricked alive so sharp
That life breathes through them from the burn-
    ing land,
And they could use the wind itself for harp
And pluck the vibrant green.

At first the whole world opens into sense:
They learn their love by looking at the wheat,
And there let fall all that was shy and tense
To walk the season slowly on propitious feet
And be all they have seen.

Now all around them earth moves toward an
    end,
The gold turning to bronze, the barley tasseled,
The fruit stored up, and soon the sheaves will
    bend
Their heads together in the rich wedding-bed
All are about to enter.

The hearts of lovers as they walk, how pure;
How cool the wind upon the open palm
As they move on toward harvest, and so sure,
Even this ripening has a marvelous calm.
And a still center.

# Leaves Before the Wind

We have walked, looking at the actual trees:
The chestnut leaves wide-open like a hand,
The beech-leaves bronzing under every breeze,
We have felt flowing through our knees
    As if we were the wind.

We have sat silent where two horses came,
Jangling their harness, to mow the long grass.
We have sat long and never found a name
For this suspension in the heart of flame
    That does not pass.

We have said nothing; we have parted often,
Not looking back, as if departure took
An absolute of will, once not again,
But this is each day's feat, as when
    The heart first shook.

Where fervor opens every instant so,
There is no instant that is not a curve,
For we are always coming as we go
And lean toward that meeting that will show
    Love's very nerve.

And so exposed (O leaves before the wind!)
We bear this flowing fire, forever free,
And learn through difficult paths to find
The whole, the center, and perhaps unbind
    The mystery,

Where there are no roots, only fervent leaves,
Nourished on meditations and the air,
Where all that comes is also all that leaves
And every hope compassionately lives
    Close to despair.

# Transition

The zinnias, ochre, orange, chrome and amber,
Fade in their cornucopia of gold,
As all the summer turns toward September
And light in torrents flows through the room.

A wasp, determined, zigzags high then low,
Hunting the bowl of rich unripened fruit,
Those purple plums clouded in powder blue,
Those pears, green-yellow with a rose high-light.

The zinnias stand so stiff they might be metal.
The wasp has come to rest on a green pear,
And as the light attacks the fruit and petal,
We sigh and feel the thunder in the air,

Who are suspended between fruit and flower;
The dying, the unripe possess our day.
By what release of will, what saving power
To taste the fruit, to throw the flowers away?

Will end of summer be the end of us?
We do not know. We simply stand and stare.
Soon they will fold and break, the metal zinnias,
The fierce wasp settle on a golden pear.

WINFIELD TOWNLEY SCOTT was born in 1910 in Haver-
hill, Mass. His published poetry includes *Mr. Whittier and
Other Poems*, *To Marry Strangers*, *The Sword on the Table*,
*Wind the Clock*, and *Biography for Traman*. He has been Phi
Beta Kappa Poet at Brown, Tufts, and Harvard; has held a
Bread Loaf fellowship, and won the Shelley Memorial Award.
At present Mr. Scott lives in Hampton, Conn., and lists his
occupation as Writer.

## Blue Sleigh

Blue sleigh that fifty winters gone
Swan-breasted heavier snows than ours,
Arrested on your summer lawn
Stands filled with earth and planted flowers.

Its shafts slant empty to the ground
As if they'd never held a horse;
Its runners make the breathless sound
Allotted rust and ghosts, of course.

The flowers are white geranium.
Stuck in June grass it looks as though
Somehow the sleigh had tunneled home
Through one immortal drift of snow.

Present preservative of past?
That what it raced through it contains?
But your illusion will not last:
Here's white geranium and it stains.

You lover of the incongruous:
Better to have your blue sleigh drawn
Through all those daisy fields across
The hills to time's malignant sun.

# Mrs. Severin

Mrs. Severin came home from the Methodist Encampment,
Climbed naked to the diningroom-table and lay down.
She was alone at the time but naturally told of it after-
ward.
'Lord! Lord!' she had called out. 'Thou seest me. Wherein
is my fault?'

When she heard of it, secondhand, Mrs. Bashfield
laughed till she cried.
'My God!' she said, 'I'd like to've watched her getting up
there!'
For Mrs. Severin, you see, was a very stout old lady,
A spilling mass by buttons, shawls, pins and ribboned
eyeglasses held together.

The eyeglasses were a shift of drama: hoisted for reading
aloud, lowered for talking;
They were not interruption. Mrs. Severin's soft incessant
sibilance
Through all the days she visited and rocked by the window
Braided inextricably Bible and Autobiography. Jesus was
near.

'The morning Encampment began the Lord suddenly
told me to go.
Ran all the way downstreet to the cars for Canobie Lake,
Didn't fasten my dress or tie my shoes. Left the house
open. Young ones at the neighbors.
"Lord," I said, "I am thy servant"—and stayed the whole
beautiful, blessed week.'

On the listening child her showers of quotation pattered
a drugged dream.
' "Thought becomes word. Word becomes act. Act be-
comes character. Character becomes destiny,"
Remember that. And praise the Lord,' she said, giving off
also
Odor of camphor, old rose jars and muttonleg sleeves.
'Amen!'

The husband long gone who wasted her inheritance; the
  irritable children
Who hated to have to have her now; the friends who took
  her in now and again: gone.
Here in her false hair and hand-me-downs, patiently talk-
  ing—talking:
Old Mrs. Severin who once, brave on a diningroom-table,
  naked confronted her unanswering Lord.

## The Difference

The buffalo loomed at the far loop of the field:
Though mildly grazing in twilight, a thunderhead teth-
  ered.
Spectators—man and two children—some others—
Clutched tickets and kept their distance, regarding the
  rare beast.

We were—after all—suddenly there—there in the same
  grass
At the edge of our town: the familiar vacant lot
Usurped by the savage shape which grazed inattentive:
We grew—embarrassed, frightened—into shy invaders.

Staring and silent, we stood back. Though the crickets
  rang
And the evening star opened low over the western fence
The shadowy field was bisontine; the ground shook—
Once—with the thud of an absent-minded forefoot.

The little girl said to her father 'I want to go see him';
But the boy dared not: he watched them hand in hand
Go slowly within the dusk to confront—quite close—
While he stayed alone among strangers—that hunching
  darkness.

Silhouette now: the buffalo: horned ghost
Of an ancient philosopher, bearded and ominous,
Transmigrated, neither free nor dead. Nothing occurred
To the father and sister. They returned safe. The three
  went home.

LOUIS SIMPSON was born in 1923 in Jamaica, British West Indies. He has published one book of verse, *The Arrivistes,* and poems by him have appeared in *Hudson Review, Partisan Review, The American Scholar, Hopkins Review,* etc. He is an Assistant Editor of the Bobbs-Merrill Company and makes his home in New York City.

## The Heroes

I dreamed of war-heroes, of wounded war-heroes
With just enough of their charms shot away
To make them more handsome. The women moved nearer
To touch their brave wounds and their hair streaked with gray.

I saw them in long ranks ascending the gang-planks;
The girls with the doughnuts were cheerful and gay.
They minded their manners and muttered their thanks;
The Chaplain advised them to watch and to pray.

They shipped these rapscallions, these sea-sick battalions
To a patriotic and picturesque spot;
They gave them new bibles and marksmen's medallions,
Compasses, maps, and committed the lot.

A fine dust has settled on all that scrap metal.
The heroes were packaged and sent home in parts
To pluck at a poppy and sew on a petal
And count the long night by the stroke of their hearts.

## The Ash and the Oak

When men discovered freedom first
The fighting was on foot,
They were encouraged by their thirst
And promises of loot,
And when it feathered and bows boomed
Their virtue was a root.

Oh, the ash and the oak and the willow tree
And green grows the grass on the infantry!

At Malplaquet and Waterloo
They were polite and proud,
They primed their guns with billets-doux
And, as they fired, bowed.
At Appomattox too, it seems
Some things were understood.

Oh, the ash and the oak and the willow tree
And green grows the grass on the infantry!

But at Verdun and at Bastogne
There was a great recoil,
The blood was bitter to the bone
The trigger to the soul,
And death was nothing if not dull
A hero was a fool.

Oh, the ash and the oak and the willow tree
And that's an end of the infantry.


## The True Weather for Women

Young women in their April moodiness
Complain of showers, for they cannot go
Swimming, or to the courts to play tennis.
But if they suffer from a gentle blow,
What will the storm, the terror of saints, do?
If April presses their green tenderness
How will they stand the full weight of the snow?

Now they are killing time, with darts and chess,
And others dancing to the radio,
And some for kisses take a turn to guess
At names, and laugh at tales of love also.
Jenny, in her hot tub, repaints a toe,
Admiring her perfect nakedness
While thunders crack and summer lightnings glow.

There is one date that they will keep, although
They have been often late to come to men,
For death hits all such deer with his long bow
And drags them by the neck into his den,
And there eternally they may complain
And tap and gesture in a frantic show
And look at summer through a windowpane.

Wind up the pulse with poppy, sleep them so!
Their selfishness will always entertain,
And even death will seem small weather woe
When love is all their sun and all their rain.
The clock will never strike, adjusted then
To their sweet drowsings, and they will not know
How punctual death is, or else how slow.

## Memories of a Lost War

The guns know what is what, but underneath
In fearful file
We go around burst boots and packs and teeth
That seem to smile.

The scene jags like a strip of celluloid.
A mortar fires.
Cinzano falls, Michelin is destroyed,
The man of tires.

As darkness drifts like fog in from the sea
Somebody says
"We're digging in." Look well, for this may be
The last of days.

Hot lightnings stitch the blind eye of the moon,
The thunder's blunt.
We sleep. Our dreams pass in a faint platoon
Toward the front.

Sleep well, for you are young. Each tree and bush
Drips with sweet dew,
And earlier than morning June's cool hush
Will waken you.

The riflemen will wake and hold their breath.
Though they may bleed
They will be proud a while of something death
Still seems to need.

## Song

Let's sing a song together once
Of Spring, when secretly
Young women dream of bulls and swans
And of one woman, I.

The flowers are a kind of game
With little lights and bells,
And I shall make them spell your name
For I love no one else.

I do not like the wind and snow,
With wind and rain I weep.
Let's sing one song before we go
And when it snows we'll sleep.

LeROY SMITH, JR., was born in Philadelphia, Pa., in 1912. He has published several chapbooks of verse, at the suggestion of Ralph Hodgson; these are entitled *Love Song of the Middle Kingdom*, *An Irish Carol*, and *Pavane;* a new book of poems, *The Fourth King*, was published by Macmillan early in 1953. Mr. Smith lives in Germantown, Pa.

⇶⇶-⇶⇶-⇶⇶-⇶⇶-⇶⇶-⇶⇶-⇶⇶-⇶⇶-⇶⇶-⇶⇶-⇶⇶⤛⤛-⤛⤛-⤛⤛-⤛⤛-⤛⤛-⤛⤛-⤛⤛-⤛⤛-⤛⤛-⤛⤛

## What Sanguine Beast?

Out of this wilderness, this stony time
Fierce with the chords of warring tigers, sick
With the shrill dissonance of dying apes
And birds, what sanguine beast shall come? shall come
And, singing, rouse again the cloven rime
That links the starlight and the winter stick,
The shaggy Adam with more seemly shapes?
What hopeful dust, and from what tomb, what tomb?

(Where Adam lies, the shreds of Christ alone,
However lustrous Adam's ruin seems,
May flesh the man of Latter Genesis,
The sanguine beast to whom the beast is known,
A dreamer in a wilderness of dreams
Dreamt as a prelude to realities.)

## Sappho Rehung

Sappho saw three stars—but, beneath their solemn
Gaze, looked purblind down; for the gift had left her,
Left her deaf-mute blind. For the gift was vision,
 Sappho was singing.

Sappho saw three stars—and remembered sorrow,
Wept for strength's frail years in her silvered weakness,
Wept for light's frail years. In her silvered darkness,
 Sappho was singing.

# Spring Song

Spring is a requiem rehearsed:
    Time's green amen
    To my decay,
    Six sparrows sing
    This bloom-glad day:
Spring is a requiem rehearsed;
I shall not hear the summer crows.
    (For dried and cracked,
    For wan and cold,
    For dull and wracked,
    For white and old,
Spring is a requiem rehearsed;
I shall not hear the summer crows.)

Spring is a dead man reimbursed:
    Six sparrows sing
    This bloom-glad day
    Time's green amen
    To my decay:
Spring is a dead man reimbursed;
I shall not walk the clover snows.
    (For dried and cracked,
    For wan and cold,
    For dull and wracked,
    For white and old,
Spring is a dead man reimbursed;
I shall not walk the clover snows.)

# Salvation Prospect

Their memories behind them
Like defeated armies,
Pharaoh and Caesar stroll
In the autumn parks of heaven,
Where the leaves are red for ever
And never fall.

146

(Oh, Pharaoh, oh, my Caesar,
Damned and forgiven,
Conscience has no eyelid,
Yet is the gift of mercy,
As also the dayglare mirror
Mirroring all.

(Oh, Pharaoh, oh, my Caesar,
Forgiven and damned,
Truth and the eye unveilèd
Fixed on her dayglare mirror
Sear with the blood's dead anguish
And, anguishing, quail.)

Their memories before them
Like returning curses,
Pharaoh and Caesar kneel
In the autumn parks of heaven,
Where the red leaves bleed for ever
And never pale.

WILLIAM JAY SMITH was born in 1918 in Winnfield, La. He has published two books: *Poems,* and *Celebration at Dark.* A Rhodes Scholar in 1947, Mr. Smith has published poetry in many periodicals, among them *Botteghe Oscure, Harper's, The New Republic,* the *Sewanee Review,* and *Poetry. Poetry* awarded him its Young Poets Prize in 1945. Mr. Smith's permanent residence is at North Pownal, Vt., where he occupies himself as writer and translator.

## *American Primitive*

Look at him there in his stovepipe hat,
His high-top shoes, and his handsome collar;
Only my Daddy could look like that,
And I love my Daddy like he loves his Dollar.

The screen door bangs, and it sounds so funny,
There he is in a shower of gold;
His pockets are stuffed with folding money,
His lips are blue, and his hands feel cold.

He hangs in the hall by his black cravat,
The ladies faint, and the children holler:
Only my Daddy could look like that,
And I love my Daddy like he loves his Dollar.

## *Processional*

The Professor strolls at dusk in the college garden,
And the hollyhocks are blooming, pink and red;
And a delicate wind is blowing, forever blowing,
In and out of the trees and through the Professor's head.

The leaves announce themselves like girls at a party,
The blades of grass stand up all fresh and trim,
While over them swing the cold, fat-bellied shadows,
And the wind goes on rehearsing an Evangelical hymn.

148

Retrace your steps, Professor. The wind in the
  branches
Blows stronger than even the Devil himself would
  wish.
The sun sinks low, the great beaked clouds assemble,
And pebbles gleam in the dark like the scales of a tropical
  fish.

And now by rush-filled pools the witches gather;
For this is the night the booming frogs foretell
When beauty will be destroyed by more than
  weather,
By more than the idiot wind that rakes the pits of Hell.

## Autumn

The color of stone when leaves are yellow,
Comes the squirrel, a capital C,
With tail atilt like a violoncello,
Comes the squirrel, musically.

Quick, quick, quick, the notes fly
Up, and off the 'cello floats
Over the lawn where children play,
Over matchstick-masted boats

Under way in the lagoon,
Down the steps, the rock walls,
Over a Triton, bearing shells,
Music flows, water falls.

Time, old hunchback, worn and yellow,
Whets his scythe on weathered stone;
While azure mists invade the hollow,
And turkey-red the leaves come down.

MARVIN SOLOMON was born in Baltimore, Md., in 1923. His poems have been published in *Commentary, Imagi, Voices, The New Yorker, Hopkins Review, The Tiger's Eye,* and *Poetry.* His first collection of poetry, *First Poems,* was published in 1952. Mr. Solomon lives in Baltimore where he is employed by a department store as a display assistant.

->>>->>>->>>->>>->>>->>>->>>->>>->>>->>>->>><<<-<<<-<<<-<<<-<<<-<<<-<<<-<<<-<<<-<<<-

## The Garden

Summer sits wilting like a lilac woman
By the wall; and cat wind
Makes a jungle of the grasses. The sun
Walks like a brilliant bird about this sundial
Of existence where shadows breathe
O'clocks. All about tall yew hedges
People the limits and trees even
Themselves against the sky; garden furniture
Ornate as grapes, clusters on the terrace,
And willows droop over the limp pool of their own
Shade. France might have carved the statuary—
And named them Versailles, or off the boulevards,
Or rich man to his mistress. . . .
In the high window and modernistic chair
Of this uncertain year, sleek and chromed
As any chair I sit trying
To allay the twitching roses
With greater distance from wire fences;
Thinking of Proust and Delius and perhaps
Corot and their small substances Sunday pierces
With its spears—radios, screen doors, and chromed voices.

## Lemon Sherbet

Unicorns move furtively among
The aspidistras, while ladies take their ices
On the terrace, cooling their thoughts
With talk of dresses

And the weather. Secret sounds
Neither summer shower nor wind, disturb the garden,
As overpopulated with flowers as
A birthday card. Jungled in

Riot cultivation, vague tigers safe
In protective coloration, seek striped shade,
Or loll royally just beyond the first
Shrubbery, eyeing the proud,

Poe-pallid women. One never senses
Husbands here, but realizes them in necessary
Offices, banked in leathers and various
Civil servants—unwary

And absent despite the danger.
For this darkened house, this terrace and terrarium are,
Like tapestries, masterpieces of dissimulation:
Nothing's really calm. The tiger

Cools, but calculates the distance
From the nearest decent cover to the nearest woman;
While she in turn represses what
The fig-leaved gods who lean

From marble pedestals suggest.
All seems surface and artistic. Only close
Examination shows the endless weaving and concealed
Design that makes the ease

And mannered attitudes seem usual:
Like the ices, everything refreshes, but is artificial.
And that is why the unicorns and tigers
Go unseen; and why the well

Brought-up but bored young lady
Excused herself from the merely elegant and clever
To take a turn about the garden,
And disappeared forever.

WALLACE STEVENS was born in Reading, Pa., in 1879. His books of poetry include *Harmonium, Ideas of Order, Owl's Clover, The Man with the Blue Guitar,* and *Auroras of Autumn.* Mr. Stevens has received various prizes and awards, including the Bollingen Prize. He has also received a number of honorary degrees. Mr. Stevens' occupation is insurance; his home in Hartford, Conn.

## Song of Fixed Accord

Rou-cou spoke the dove,
Like the sooth lord of sorrow,
Of sooth love and sorrow,
And a hail-bow, hail-bow,
To this morrow.

She lay upon the roof,
A little wet of wing and woe,
And she rou-ed there,
Softly she piped among the suns
And their ordinary glare,

The sun of five, the sun of six,
Their ordinariness,
And the ordinariness of seven,
Which she accepted,
Like a fixed heaven,

Not subject to change.
Day's invisible beginner,
The lord of love and of sooth sorrow,
Lay on the roof
And made much within her.

# Two Illustrations That the World
## Is What You Make of It

### I

#### THE CONSTANT DISQUISITION OF THE WIND

The sky seemed so small that winter day,
A dirty light on a lifeless world,
Contracted like a withered stick.

It was not the shadow of cloud and cold,
But a sense of the distance of the sun—
The shadow of a sense of his own,

A knowledge that the actual day
Was so much less. Only the wind
Seemed large and loud and high and strong.

And as he thought within the thought
Of the wind, not knowing that that thought
Was not his thought, nor anyone's,

The appropriate image of himself,
So formed, became himself and he breathed
The breath of another nature as his own,

But only its momentary breath,
Outside of and beyond the dirty light,
That never could be animal,

A nature still without a shape,
Except his own—perhaps, his own
In a Sunday's violent idleness.

### II

#### THE WORLD IS LARGER IN SUMMER

He left half a shoulder and half a head
To recognize him in after time.

These marbles lay weathering in the grass
When the summer was over, when the change

Of summer and of the sun, the life
Of summer and of the sun, were gone.

He had said that everything possessed
The power to transform itself, or else,

And what meant more, to be transformed.
He discovered the colors of the moon

In a single spruce, when, suddenly,
The tree stood dazzling in the air

And blue broke on him from the sun,
A bullioned blue, a blue abulge,

Like daylight, with time's bellishings,
And sensuous summer stood full-height.

The master of the spruce, himself,
Became transformed. But his mastery

Left only the fragments found in the grass,
From his project, as finally magnified.

## Prologues to What Is Possible

### I

There was an ease of mind that was like being alone in a
boat at sea,
A boat carried forward by waves resembling the bright
backs of rowers,
Gripping their oars, as if they were sure of the way to
their destination,
Bending over and pulling themselves erect on the wooden
handles,
Wet with water and sparkling in the oneness of their
motion.

The boat was built of stones that had lost their weight
and being no longer heavy
Had left in them only a brilliance, of unaccustomed
origin,

So that he that stood up in the boat leaning and looking
  before him
Did not pass like someone voyaging out of and beyond
  the familiar.
He belonged to the far-foreign departure of his vessel and
  was part of it,
Part of the speculum of fire on its prow, its symbol, what-
  ever it was,
Part of the glass-like sides on which it glided over the
  salt-stained water,

As he traveled alone, like a man lured on by a syllable
  without any meaning,
A syllable of which he felt, with an appointed sureness,
That it contained the meaning into which he wanted to
  enter,
A meaning which, as he entered it, would shatter the
  boat and leave the oarsmen quiet
As at a point of central arrival, an instant moment, much
  or little,
Removed from any shore, from any man or woman, and
  needing none.

## II

The metaphor stirred his fear. The object with which he
  was compared
Was beyond his recognizing. By this he knew that likeness
  of him extended
Only a little way, and not beyond, unless between himself
And things beyond resemblance there was this and that
  intended to be recognized,
The this and that in the enclosures of hypotheses
On which men speculated in summer when they were
  half asleep.

What self, for example, did he contain that had not yet
  been loosed,
Snarling in him for discovery as his attentions spread,
As if all his hereditary lights were suddenly increased
By an access of color, a new and unobserved, slight dith-
  ering,

The smallest lamp, which added its puissant flick, to
   which he gave
A name and privilege over the ordinary of his common-
   place—

A flick which added to what was real and its vocabulary,
The way some first thing coming into Northern trees
Adds to them the whole vocabulary of the South,
The way the earliest single light in the evening sky, in
   spring,
Creates a fresh universe out of nothingness by adding
   itself,
The way a look or a touch reveals its unexpected
   magnitudes.

ELEANOR GLENN (Mrs. Hayward) WALLIS was born in Baltimore, Md., where she still lives. She has published several books of poetry—*Child on a Mill-Farm, Natural World, Tidewater Country,* and *Design for an Arras.* She has won awards from *Voices, Wings, Contemporary Poetry,* and the Poetry Society of Georgia.

>>>->>>->>>->>>->>>->>>->>>->>>->>>->>>>-<<<-<<<-<<<-<<<-<<<-<<<-<<<-<<<-<<<-<<<-

## The Deathless Ones

They have vanished, the immortal horses of Achilles,
   Have left no trace behind
Save hoofmarks on the pages of great Homer
   Who was blind.

Sired by the Westwind, foaled by that winged harpy,
   Podarge the wilful one,
They were yoked to the chariot of Patroklos
   By Automodon.

Their running-mate, the mortal steed Pedasus,
   Met that day a fatal thrust
By the shoulder wound that threw him from his traces
   To the dust.

Though Pedasus died of spear-thrust and Patroklos
   In his own blood bathed,
Xanthus, Balios, the immortal horses,
   Went unscathed.

But they sorrowed for the slaying of Patroklos,
   Each with lowered head
As great tears fell from the eyes of these immortals
   For the dead.

# "Trade" Rat

## Neotoma Cinerea

Now, like a magpie, he collects the bright,
The portable object as he steals about
Furred in warm yellow, throat and belly white.
He is no thief. Each trinket is replaced
By one of value to himself, no doubt;
His honesty and guile are interlaced.

His tiny house is lined with feathers, fur
And everything that glitters. By and by,
The fragment of red glass, the cockleburr,
Will be exchanged for one smooth silver coin.
Decreased in value to his trader's eye,
This too shall go for what he may purloin.

His house, well-roofed with cactus spine and thorn,
Is floored with cedar. In it he can rest
When winter makes the outer world forlorn.
Nor does he hibernate. Without a store
Of fat, he waits until the storm has passed
And he can find a nut or two once more.

His lengthy whisker quivers and his eye,
White-rimmed and brilliant, scans the moonlit
    tree,
The ground beneath. He skitters to the high,
Ascending trunk and out upon a limb,
From which depends the scented nut that he
Detaches from the twig that beckons him.

This hunger being filled, he seeks again
To satisfy a craving subtler far,
To barter what he has for what he fain
Would use to make a palace of his slums,
So steals about by light of moon or star
Till glitter calls to him and he succumbs.

JOHN HALL WHEELOCK was born in Far Rockaway, N. Y., in 1886. In addition to numerous books of poetry, *The Human Fantasy, The Beloved Adventure, Love and Liberation, Dust and Light, The Black Panther, The Bright Doom,* and *Poems, 1911-1936,* Mr. Wheelock edited *Editor to Author: the Letters of Maxwell E. Perkins,* and *The Face of a Nation: Poetical Passages from the Writings of Thomas Wolfe.* A member of the National Institute of Arts and Letters, he lives in New York City, and is an editor with Charles Scribner's Sons.

## Valediction

Glory of soundless heaven, wheel of stars
Round the bright axle-tree in silence turning!
Trellis and cloudy vine! Great labyrinth
And wilderness of light! Hear, you proud flames
Hung high forever, your cold Medusa stare
Has turned a heart to stone.

## Random Reflections on a Cloudless Sunday

Gulls, that live by the water and hang around docks,
    Know about fish, how to fetch them out of the sea—
They know, also, how to split clams on rocks,
    But nothing (and this gives them a certain dignity)
About "the seriousness of the present world situation."

The squirrel, that is so clever at cracking a nut
    And indulges in such fascinating antics,
Can walk, head first, down the trunk of a tree, but
    Knows little, if anything, about semantics.
The impression he leaves with me is rather a pleasant one.

159

There is an alligator lives in the Zoo
   Who is gifted, though he neither paints nor sings—
He has made an art of having nothing better to do,
   Never gets nervous or "takes a grave view of things."
I find him, for some reason or other, extremely attractive.

Do you think the world will end with a bang or a whim-
   per?
   I'm rather inclined to think it won't end with a bang—
More probably with a simper,
   Like that on the face of the little orang-outang
In Bronx Park when he's feeling so pleased with himself.

## Prayer

Have pity on us, Power just and severe,
   Have pity on our greed, our hate, our lust,
And on our endless anxieties, our ugly fear.
   Great Wisdom, grant wisdom to this timid dust.

Have patience with us, who have betrayed one
   another
   And parted the single and seamless robe of
   man,
And divided his garments among us, who is our
   brother.
   Infinite Patience, have patience if You can.

Have mercy on us—because we are merciless
   And have need of mercy, all other needs
   above—
And on our angry littleness,
   Pity Inexorable, Remorseless Love.

## Wood-Thrush

Behind the wild-bird's throat
An Eden, more remote
Than Adam knew of, lies—
The primal paradise,

Lost, yet forever here,
From that wild syrinx cries,
Into the listening ear
The labyrinthine heart,
A longing, a regret,
In which it has no part.
Where the young leaves are met
In overarching green
Soft winds stir and divide,
Where shadows cloud and throng
The coverts in between,
That early bud of song
Opens its petals wide,
Becomes a threefold star
Of voices twined and blent,
Happy and innocent,
Within whose singing are
Troy lost and Hector slain,
Judas and Golgotha,
The longing and the pain,
Sorrows of old that were
And joy come back again
From ages earlier,
Before joy's course was run,
Before time's bounds were set—
The fountains of the sun
Are in that tiny jet
Of song, so clear, so cool.
While the false heart raves on,
For longing, like a fool,
The quiet voice is gone:
The song inept to save,
Happy and innocent,
Falls silent as the grave,
Closing the door upon
Those half-remembered things—

RICHARD WILBUR was born in New York City in 1921. His books are *The Beautiful Changes* and *Ceremony and Other Poems*. Mr. Wilbur has won the Harriet Monroe and Oscar Blumenthal prizes and holds a Guggenheim Fellowship for the current year. His home is in Lincoln, Mass.; he gives his occupation as teacher.

⇒⇒-⇒⇒-⇒⇒-⇒⇒-⇒⇒-⇒⇒-⇒⇒-⇒⇒-⇒⇒⇐⇐-⇐⇐-⇐⇐-⇐⇐-⇐⇐-⇐⇐-⇐⇐-⇐⇐-⇐⇐

## After the Last Bulletins

After the last bulletins the windows darken
And the whole city founders easily and deep,
Sliding on all its pillows
To the thronged Atlantis of personal sleep,

And the wind rises. The wind rises and bowls
The day's litter of news in the alleys. Trash
Tears itself on the railings,
Soars and falls with a soft crash,

Tumbles and soars again. In empty lots
Our journals spiral in a fierce noyade
Of all we thought to think,
Or caught in corners cramp and wad

And twist our words. And some from gutters flail
Their tatters at the tired patrolman's feet
Like all that fisted snow
That cried beside his long retreat

Damn you! damn you! to the emperor's horses'
    heels.
Oh none too soon through the air white and dry
Will the clear announcer's voice
Beat like a dove, and you and I

From the heart's anarch and responsible town
Rise by the subway-mouth to life again,
Bearing the morning papers,
And cross the park where saintlike men,

White and absorbed, with stick and bag remove
The litter of the night, and footsteps rouse
With confident morning sound
The songbirds in the public boughs.

## Beasts

Beasts in their major freedom
Slumber in peace tonight. The gull on his ledge
Dreams in the guts of himself the moon-plucked waves
        below,
And the sunfish leans on a stone, slept
        By the lyric water;

In which the spotless feet
Of deer make dulcet splashes, and to which
The ripped mouse, safe in the owl's talon, cries
        Concordance. Here there is no such harm
        And no such darkness

As the selfsame moon observes
Where, warped in window-glass, it sponsors now
The werewolf's painful change. Turning his head away
        On the sweaty bolster, he tries to remember
        The mood of manhood,

But lies at last, as always,
Letting it happen, the fierce fur soft to his face,
Hearing with sharper ears the wind's exciting minors,
        The leaves' panic, and the degradation
        Of the heavy streams.

Meantime, at high windows
Far from thicket and pad-fall, suitors of excellence
Sigh and turn from their work to construe again the
        painful
Beauty of heaven, the lucid moon
        And the risen hunter,

Making such dreams for men
As told will break their hearts as always, bringing
Monsters into the city, crows on the public statues,
        Navies fed to the fish in the dark
        Unbridled waters.

# Apology

A word sticks in the wind's throat;
A wind-launch drifts in the swells of rye;
Sometimes, in broad silence,
The hanging apples distil their darkness.

You, in a green dress, calling, and with brown hair,
Who come by the field-path now, whose name I
say
Softly, forgive me love if also I call you
Wind's word, apple-heart, haven of grasses.

# Speech for the Repeal of
# the McCarran Act

As Wulfstan said on another occasion,
The strong net bellies in the wind and
the spider rides it out;
But history, that sure blunderer,
Ruins the unkempt web, however silver.

I am not speaking of rose windows
Shattered by bomb-shock, the leads touseled;
the glass-grains broadcast;
If the rose be living at all
A gay gravel shall be pollen of churches.

Nor do I mean railway networks.
Torn-up tracks are no great trouble. As
Wulfstan said,
It is oathbreach, faithbreach, lovebreach
Brings the invaders into the estuaries.

Shall one man drive before him ten
Unstrung from sea to sea? Let thought be
free. I speak
Of the spirit's weaving, the neural
Web, the self-true mind, the trusty reflex.

WILLIAM CARLOS WILLIAMS was born in 1883. He has written short stories, novels, and an autobiography in addition to his poems, which include complete collections of both early and late poems, and the long poem, *Paterson*. Dr. Williams holds honorary degrees from the University of Buffalo, Bard College, Rutgers, and the University of Pennsylvania. He has won many awards, the Guarantors' Prize of Poetry in 1931, the Dial Award in 1926, the Loines Award, 1948, the National Book Award in 1950, and, most recently, the Bollingen Prize for 1952. Dr. Williams is by profession a physician, living in Rutherford, N. J., his native town.

>>>->>>->>>->>>->>>->>>->>>->>>->>>>|<<<-<<<-<<<-<<<-<<<-<<<-<<<-<<<-<<<-<<<

## *To a Dog Injured in the Street*

IT IS MYSELF,
  not the poor beast lying there
    yelping with pain
that brings me to myself with a start—
  as at the explosion
    of a bomb, a bomb that has laid

all the world waste.
  I can do nothing
    but sing about it
and so I am assuaged
  from my pain.

A DROWSY NUMBNESS drowns my sense
  as if of hemlock
    I had drunk. I think
of the poetry
  of René Char
    and all he must have seen

and suffered
  that has brought him
    to speak only of

sedgy rivers,
                of daffodils and tulips
                        whose roots they water,
even to the freeflowing river
                that laves the rootlets
                        of those sweet scented flowers
that people the
                milky
                        way.
I REMEMBER *Norma*
                our English setter of my childhood
                        her silky ears
and expressive eyes.
                She had a litter
                        of pups one night
in our pantry and I kicked
                one of them
                        thinking, in my alarm,
that they
                were biting her breasts
                        to destroy her.
I REMEMBER also
                a dead rabbit
                        lying harmlessly
on the outspread palm
                of a hunter's hand.
                        As I stood by
watching
                he took a hunting knife
                        and with a laugh
thrust it
                up into the animal's private parts.
                I almost fainted.
WHY SHOULD I think of that now?
                the cries of a dying dog
                        are to be blotted out
as best I can.
                René Char
                        you are a poet who believes

in the power of beauty
            to right all wrongs.
                    I believe it also.
With invention and courage
        we shall surpass
                the pitiful dumb beasts,
let all men believe it,
            as you have taught me also
                    to believe it.

EDMUND WILSON was born in Red Bank, N. J., in 1895.
America's most highly praised critic, he has also written plays,
a novel, *I Thought of Daisy,* and short stories, and published
two books of verse, *Poets, Farewell,* and *Note-Books of Night.*
Mr. Wilson's home is at Wellfleet on Cape Cod; he has re-
cently been a visiting lecturer at Princeton.

—»»—»»—»»—»»—»»—»»—»»—»»—»»—»»«««—«««—«««—«««—«««—«««—«««—«««—«««—«««—

# *The White Sand*

Slender I saw her stand, stooped a little, her arms akimbo,
    Tall and tapering-limbed, half pigeon-toed on the sand;

Shy but so sure of her beauty that, bare on the beach in
    the sunlight,
    Smart as a Paris gown, clothed her from head to foot;

Eyes drafts of daylight illumined, as noon does a tropical
    harbor,
    Bright with the beams it absorbs, burning miraculous
    blue,

Bending that quick German kindness, that clearness of
    Russian perception:
    Birch-dwellers' limpid depth, flood that affirms of the
    Rhine.

Slender she moved and slipped in—a water-diviner's osier:
    Tiny diminishing toes, dipping brown head, the pale
    skin—

Passing our sunburned sprawlers splashing, with scarcely
    a ripple,
    Plying from little hips, loping a lazy crawl,

Lifting lithe angular arms, as her slow easy-reaching
    strokes fell.
    Touched with delight, I looked, suddenly calmed and
    charmed;

Followed her, floating alone, as she lost herself, fluent in
  fluid—
  White that was balanced in blue—shoulders that
  scarcely shone;

Watched her as, rising, she waded, alighting, a snowy
  egret,
  Stepping on slim heron legs, foreign but unafraid,

Folded her wings, still wet—her quietness made me
  silent—
  Dropped to her knees and smiled, asked for a cigarette.

Silent I long remained while there lingered from every
  meeting
  Grace that turned staleness sweet, peace that remitted
  pain,

Shed by blue glance and bland brow, where all that was
  simple was noble;
  Nothing subtle, for show; all that was gentle, proud.

These in firm stead would have stood me—a wonder half-
  dreamed, had they ended
  Hardly the murmur of friends meeting for menu food;

Fearing to follow, to love you, these I still kept in de-
  parting:
  Half-shade of Fragonard bluing the green of a grove;

Song that pours plaintive or gay from Schubert's blue-
  coated Vienna:
  Lindens and lonely men, millers and brooks and May;

Voice of an eager Rostóv, alive in his limitless country
  Moist with the smell of the hunt—calling and gallop-
  ing off—

Metaphors all that must fail me—since shadow must stay
  for the painter,
  Melodies pivot in change, pages repeat their tale.

Style bestowed not by skill only, amazing, may modulate
  —living,
  Flushing and fugitive—flesh on its trellis of bone—

Tune the soft flow of the waistline to deep-throated
 intonations,
 Shape to the high-ribbed face rondures of shoulder
  and breast,

Lighting, perceived, a pure image that pulses, that hovers,
 consoling—
 Brightening, even remote, memory hardly dimmed.

Sands that had darkened I lost them—woods that had
 wasted I left them—
 Rubble and splinters to sift, rocking horizons cross;

Then with the white sands refound you in first days of
 fondness and summer:
 High in our white-walled room, hardly an August
  sound

Brushed to us, buried, embosomed in pale privet-blos-
 soms, pink ramblers,
 Quietly stirring or calm; guarded by gables that rose

Green from the greenery, marshes beyond, that lay rip-
 pling and silky,
 Rimmed by the woody low hills, houses white cubes
  cut sharp;

Lunching on sliced delicious cucumbers, roucoucouling
 Pigeons in eaves, with the cool nimbus of wine well-
  iced.

Noons when our blond boys were playing in sea without
 surf, we slumbered,
 Salt-steeped and sun-benumbed, sunk in the sand of
  the Bay;

Moments when, moving at leisure, you rose, at once lis-
 some and gawky,
 Languid I watched you stalk, blond on the zinc-blond
  sea.

Those were the days when the sun and the sea and the
 wine were a pressure
 Fusing partitions of flesh, forcing new blood to run;

Those were the days when I tasted you—tender as white
   osetrína.
Firm as sea-flavored blin melting in delicate paste,

Mousse of fresh strawberries frozen in smooth inexhausti-
   ble portions,
   Palpitant pools of borscht creaming rich crimson rose,

Cream-stirred kisél that keeps tartness—those were the
   days when I drank you:
   Pétillant Rheims champagne ripened by Rhenish art,

Slender long-shouldered hock—those were the days when
   I, feasting,
   Summoned a second guest, shouldered from broader
   stock,

Yellow-haired, blue-eyed blondínka, who, stubborn, sure-
   fingered, sure-footed,
   Pushed at the door still shut, rattled the knob to
   come in.

Blue plates with scalloped gilt edges deployed in the
   plate-racks, disclosing
   Violet, crocus and rose, purple and lemon and red;

Middle room bloomed pinks and blues; pink fuchsias
   bedecked a brick terrace,
   Littered with long summer chairs. Summer was brisk
   and confused:

Sand in the beds—I but brushed you, when brayings of
   radio'd ballgames,
   Bangings of bedroom brawls, had to be heard and
   hushed;

Dogs driven in from the moon and the dust where they
   basked, barking:
   Doors latched and rooms made dark—dumb, we sub-
   sided soon.

Winter was quiet and bright—with the sea-going throb
   of the burner,
   Chekhov read out by turn, stumbling—you lay at night

Slim in your linen sheets, pink-comfortered, propped in
   plump pillows,
   Smiling and kind and still, smooth and gardenia-sweet.

Silence was never a tension nor ever was movement dis-
   union:
   Climbing October dunes, skirting November fens,

Threading twig-brittle forests—a touch or a word would
   reach you.
   Once on a narrow beach, wild as our outer shore

Wintering bleakly, but cozily hidden, hemmed in by the
   pinewoods,
   Drowsy with walking and wine, hugging the sun, you
   dozed;

Drenched from the opposite bank, a shadow that, black
   and opaque, lay
   Deeper it seemed than the lake, daunting the mind
   with its blank,

Toward me, devouring but faceless, advanced—till it
   darkly reflected—
   Ochre-patched, pallid-streaked—headlong the humped
   pine-mass,

Marbling with objects seen that menace—then, mirror-
   wise spreading
   Painting cordovan red, golden and tan and green,

Stabilized, glazing unbroken, a world hardly skimmed by
   a ripple
   Slow as the pulse of sleep—brisker it widened—you
   woke,

Wakening love, our dear love, that pushed firm on the
   sand, among writhen
   Whitening limbs of no pith—pines on the high bank
   above

Brushwood and scrub lifted nobler antlers, extending
   their lofty
   Furry and phallic tufts—silver, the molten globe

Spilled on the western ridge—a bird throbbed—I lay in fainting
   Pleasure—a purring plane blemished the blue, a midge.

So by the pool of my solitude, gasping in brackish waters,
   Lethargies smothering thought, stupors that scarcely brood,

Easily sliding a shade, you showed me the screen of appearance,
   Picturing, terraced and clear, station and race and trade;

Set me to pore on, unwind it, reweave it, expand its dimensions:
   Tessaract-tissue of sense, intellect—two undefined

Others—"love"? "beauty"?—Oh, wonder that held me! Oh, image that brightened
   Seasons of barren spite—borne from the summer pond!

Pledged to this world you restore, have you passed into all with your blessing:
   Orchards and Chekhov and chess, children and bed and board?

Pliant, providing, pervading, evasive, decisive in vagueness—
   Bowing, you disobey; vanishing, do not fade—

Spirit as fleet as that fairy that flies to men's need in the fable,
   Balming the birth-cursed babe—Iris of light and air!

Suddenly turning my eyes, I find myself safe in your presence,
   Rhine-daughter, northern princess, always with fresh surprise—

Dreaming still—hardly believed, half known, hardly there to revisit,
   Save as such verses as these features and form may give—

Fresh for me still in its essence, that shore where your
  high little instep—
Printing white sand, the fair skin—blue-veined and
  curved, has pressed.

SAMUEL YELLEN was born in Vilna, Lithuania, in 1906. He has contributed poems, stories, and sketches to *The New Yorker,* the *Atlantic Monthly, Antioch Review, The American Scholar,* and other publications; his first book of poetry, *In the House and Out, and Other Poems,* appeared in 1952. **Mr.** Yellen is Professor of English at Indiana University and editor of the Indiana University Poetry Series. He lives in Bloomington.

## Prognostic

There comes a moment late in Summer
When yellow pulses like a muffled bell,
A tremor foreboding the mortal stroke,
The first faltering of the chlorophyll.

This is not the yellow haunting the mind
In ghost of crocus, daffodil, lemon-bright
Forsythia, new butter of the daisy disk,
Yellow dissolving light, dissolved in light.

That airy yellow, cream yellow, flaxen yellow,
Spirit yellow washed pale gold by the Spring sun,
Together with flesh of primrose, jonquil, butter-
    cup,
Has long since drowned in a heavy sea of green.

No, this yellow is waxen, tawny, buff,
Mottled gold of straw, wheat stalk, corn husk:
Darkness is a presence, fog an interfusion—
This is antique amber holding an inner dusk.

There comes a moment when thought reverberates
And yellow is a passing bell; indeed, tomorrow
Stains the world hectic, speckles it with red fever,
Then wastes and crumples it to dry brown sorrow.

# The Cloisters

*Fort Tryon Park, New York*

Here in the Cloisters a fourth dimension evolves,
A remote time–place of monk, knight, and herald;
Here other men once made *their* peace with the world,
And that much harder peace, peace with themselves.

Today I walk alone in the silence almost heard,
The seven-century hush transported stone by stone
To this alien ground. I listen here alone,
The little fountain trills the clear song of a bird.

Though much here is "restored," much remains the same:
Carved angel, beast, placid and tormented soul
Gaze down from corbel, lintel, capital
Upon the same fevered flesh in frantic search of balm.

The cloister flowers, blue, gold, purple, pink and white,
Are those once stained in glass, woven in tapestries—
Jonquils, hyacinths, daisies, violets, fleurs-de-lys,
The colors somewhat slack in this less brilliant light.

Through the western arches, as in painted fantasy,
Beyond the broad Hudson's rippling sheens and shades
Rise the riven rusts of the sculptured Palisades,
And there for perspective against the sky a gull soars free.

Oh, I, I am a cheerless captive the cloister stones embrace.
I touch one stone decayed, not by time nor rain,
But by ingesting sorrow, passion, guilt, and pain,
A stone worn soft and gentle as a human face.

The sour corrupting acids are sucked up from my breast.
Who gives me this stone gives me a healing herb
With infinite capacity to draw out and absorb:
A smile denotes the cheerless captive become the cheer-
  ful guest.

# The Wooden Tiger

This tiger is not Blake's tiger burning bright:
Some *mortal* hand framed this fearful symmetry,
Hewed and whittled out of wood this life-size counterfeit.
And wood is not a bad kind of flesh, being free
Of rapid depreciation by animal chemistry.

The model was no domesticated pussycat,
But the real thing in total recall down to vibrant tail.
The cunning hand made use of woody grain, whorl, knot,
To hint at muscle, rib, and haunch-bone, all carved to
     scale,
Eight savage feet from whiskered nose to tip of tail.

A century has not slackened the wide cruel grin;
And while some seams have given along the sides and
     back,
The undimmed colors still ring out, the rufous brown
To burn through green leaves, the white cheeks and belly,
     the black
Traverse stripes arching down and under from the back.

This is a dread man-eater. The evidence is clear.
The teeth are worn and defective, and one stump is gone.
But most conclusive, the hand that worked with loving
     care
Has been swallowed up, bequeathing us this cryptic
     yawn—
At least there is no doubt the mortal hand is gone.

Yes, the hand which forged the wood by oil or candle-
     light,
Bodying forth into view and thus putting out of mind
What burned and flickered there in the phosphorescent
     night,
Has long since disappeared, yet prankishly left behind
This beast denied forever the forests of the mind.

And now the wooden tiger, come far from its last kill,
Haunts our little clearing on the outskirts of the jungle,

No longer gratified by wild hog, deer, or peafowl.
If it would pounce and strike, we could trust it not to
    bungle;
But it prowls forever powerless, cut off from its jungle.

## *Discourse on the Real*

The shades are half-drawn on classroom and hall
Now deserted but for the ghostly babel
Left by the celebrants in the perennial miracle
Of Alphabet and Multiplication Table:
On a back door, to *épater le bourgeois*,
One Summer infidel has fixed the taunting scribble
*School is over school is over ha ha ha!*

Not long since the schoolyard cradled a little nation,
The sole material residue of former act and cry
Being the crumpled dusty wrappers in gentle
    gyration
Of Baby Ruth, Wild Cherry Gum, and Eskimo Pie.
But off there, sunlight and air currents beget swarms
Of leaping shapes and phantoms to trick the eye,
A whirling dance of Platonic Ideas or Forms.

And now I make out Coquetry in a dress's flutter,
And Love strolls hand-in-hand along the walks;
There Indecision goes up and down on the
    teeter-totter,
And Master Builder raises castles in the sandbox.
Exhibition throws himself from ring to ring,
While False Modesty stands aside and mutely mocks,
And Dreamer rides to Graustark on her private
    swing.

The sun strikes untold colors from the play-
    ground pebbles.
I shake the fictive from my head: the schoolhouse
    brick
Is plain and real and solid, fact not fable—
No need for Dr. Johnson's confirming kick.

And yet, I think, the filling matter is the fiction,
The leaping shapes and phantoms not a trick;
Perhaps we find the real in the abstraction.

Always there will be the new First Grader,
Although the particular flesh that took the mold
Has gone on down the years wiser and sadder:
The forms are always with us waiting to be filled.
And always the bushes screening the steps conceal
The ever-present Platonist sitting there, beguiled
By which of this is fiction, which is real.

# About the Editor

Rolfe Humphries has been distinguished among American poets ever since his first book of verse appeared in 1929. He has since published four more books of poetry: *Out of the Jewel* (1942); *The Summer Landscape* (1945); *Forbid Thy Ravens* (1947); and *The Wind of Time* (1949).

No less esteemed as a translator, Mr. Humphries has made a highly regarded English version of *The Aeneid* (1950). His most recent work in this field is *The Gypsy Ballads of Garcia Lorca*, published by Indiana University Press (1953).

Critic and teacher of writing too, Mr. Humphries has for years conducted the Verse Chronicle department of The Nation, and at various times has been on the faculties of the Writers' Conferences at the University of New Hampshire, Indiana University, and the University of Colorado. Among his honors are a Guggenheim Fellowship, a Shelley Memorial Award, the Poetry Awards Prize, and an honorary Master of Arts degree from his Alma Mater, Amherst College. He has recently been elected a member of the National Institute of Arts and Letters.

Mr. Humphries' vocation is teacher of Latin at an academy on Long Island, where he also assists in the coaching of football.